# MODERN U.S. NAVY
# SUBMARINES

## Robert and Robin Genat

MBI Publishing Company

# DEDICATION

To
Creighton Laskey,
my one and only, best kid ever.
Love, Mom

First published in 1997 by MBI Publishing Company, 729 Prospect Avenue, PO Box 1, Osceola, WI 54020-0001 USA

MBI Publishing Company books are also available at discounts in bulk quantity for industrial or sales-promotional use. For details write to Special Sales Manager at Motorbooks International Wholesalers & Distributors, 729 Prospect Avenue, PO Box 1 Osceola, WI 54020-0001 USA

Library of Congress Cataloging-in-Publication Data
Genat, Robert.
        Modern US Navy submarines/ Robert Genat & Robin Genat.
             p.  cm.-- (Enthusiast color series)
        Includes index.
        ISBN 0-7603-0276-6 (alk. paper)
        1. Submarines (Ships)--United States. I. Genat, Robin, 1948-
        II. Title. III. Series.
        V858.G46 1997                   97-8680
        359.9'3'0973--dc21

**On the front cover:** USS CHICAGO (SSN-721) has just returned from a 6-month patrol. The traditional red, white, and blue Hawaiian lei is still draped over the sail. Most crew members have left with family members and loved ones. But the submarine is never left unattended—watches are stood around the clock.

**On the frontispiece:** A planesman controls the up and down movements of the dive planes on the sail of USS OHIO (SSBN-726). Generally one of the youngest members of the crew, he is closely supervised by senior crew members just behind him in the Control Center.

**On the title page:** A Change of Command Ceremony takes place aboard USS SALT LAKE CITY (SSN-716) at Naval Submarine Base, San Diego, California. The intent of this simple ceremony is to transfer total responsibility, authority, and accountability from one individual to another. The procedure was designed to ensure that only the authorized officer held command and that all aboard were aware of the authenticity of his orders.

**On the back cover:** USS ALASKA (SSBN-732) waits patiently for buoyancy as water is pumped into the dry dock at Naval Submarine Base, Bangor, Washington.

Edited by Michael Haenggi
Designed by Katie Finney

Printed in Hong Kong

# CONTENTS

# ACKNOWLEDGMENTS

I was up to about page 50 of James Calvert's book, *Surface at the Pole: The Extraordinary Voyages of the USS Skate.* Calvert is the well-known author of numerous classics about submarines and a former commanding officer. My eyes widened in astonishment as the author began to describe one of the officers under his command on this historic voyage—CDR John Nicholson.

CDR Nicholson had been one of the top men in his class at Annapolis and one of the first submarine officers hand-picked by Rickover for training in nuclear power. He was the XO and Navigation Officer aboard USS SKATE (SSN-578), assigned to navigate the dangerous ice floes of the Arctic Ocean in 1959. Could this be the same (now Vice Admiral) Nicholson to whom we had been introduced when we first began to think about this book project? Was this the same Nicholson selected for the first cruise of USS NAUTILUS (SSN-571), the world's first nuclear powered submarine? It was! I was beginning to feel small and insignificant.

Thank you, Admiral Nicholson, for being our advocate for this project. You pointed us in the right direction, introduced us to the right people, and made a phone call or two when necessary. We stand in awe of you and your fellow submariners.

We'd also like to thank Lt. Danny Hernandez for getting us our necessary submarine embarks and for putting up with our nagging and pestering. A huge thank you to PAOs Paul Taylor and LCDR Dave Lee at Naval Submarine Base, Bangor, Washington. In addition to giving us information on Trident submarines, we learned about native plants, clam digging, and wild deer.

It was in Bangor that we began to understand the role of understatement in the submarine community. "Your ride on the Alaska's been canceled," we were informed. Why? we ask. "Submarine broke." And on a later occasion we asked, "How come the Alaska's not coming out of drydock tonight, as scheduled?" "No place to go," was the response from a chief walking along the drydock. I guess that's all we needed to know.

Thanks to everyone who told us all we needed to know.

Vice Admiral John H. Nicholson, USN (Retired); Captain Thomas L. Travis, Commander Submarine Squadron Eleven (6/94-7/96); Lt. Danny Hernandez, PAO, COMSUBPAC Rep West Coast; LCDR Dave Lee, PAO, Naval Submarine Base Bangor, Washington; Paul Taylor, PAO, Bangor, Washington; MMC (SS) Allen J. Keyser, Trident Training Facility, Bangor, Washington; Commander W.M. Smith, USS JEFFERSON CITY (SSN-759); Commander David M. Schubert, USS CHICAGO (SSN-721); Commander Walter H. Yourstone, USS OHIO (SSBN-726) Gold; MMCM (SS) Conrad J. Gillaspie, Chief of the Boat, USS CHICAGO (SSN-721); ETCM (SS) R.D. West, Chief of the Boat, USS PORTSMOUTH (SSN-707); YN2 (SS) Gary Wallis, PAO, USS OHIO (SSBN-726) Gold; ETC (SS/SW) Gene Brockington, Submarine Group Eleven, San Diego, California; Captain J. Denver McCune, Past President, Pacific Southwest Chapter Naval Submarine League (USN, Retired); William Kenny, Public Affairs Officer, Naval Submarine School, Groton, Connecticut; LCDR Robert D. Raine, PAO, Naval Submarine Base, King's Bay, Georgia; Lisa L. Trolan, Public Relations, Electric Boat; and Russell D. Egnor, Director, News Photo Division, Navy Office of Information.

# INTRODUCTION

In a narrow passageway on Level One just below the sail, the Executive Officer of the nuclear attack submarine USS CHICAGO (SSN-721) strapped me into a bright red nylon body harness for my trip topside into the open air. I put one foot onto the first rung of a stainless steel ladder and began my vertical climb toward a small circular patch of blue sky. I struggled out of the hatch and was blasted with cool fresh air and the sound of a surging sea as the blunt bow of the sub plowed through the surface of the Pacific Ocean off the coast of San Diego, California.

Secured by a length of rope to a temporary railing around the top of the sail, I gaped at the view. At 18 knots, the dome-shaped bow, 33 feet across, peeled back the surface of the ocean creating an immense transparent sheet of green water. Astern, the wake stretched for miles. Three seagulls had hitched a ride on the warm black aft deck of the CHICAGO, their feet cushioned by acoustic tiles on the skin of the boat.

The American flag snapped furiously as if it would break loose. What a great looking flag! I was standing on top of the world, and on the wings of another man's dream—a modern U.S. nuclear-powered attack submarine.

In the early 1950s, Hyman G. Rickover, then a Captain in the U.S. Navy, was part of a small group of naval officers who understood what could be done with a nuclear-powered submarine. Imagine not having to refuel. Imagine not having to surface for fresh air. Imagine being able to disappear for long periods of time, your whereabouts unknown. The introduction of nuclear power changed forever the nature of submarine warfare. Rickover championed this vision until he got what he wanted and

remained the guardian of America's nuclear Navy until his retirement in 1982.

The landmark event in this transition to a new era was the sailing of the first nuclear-powered submarine, USS NAUTILUS (SSN-571), on 17 January 1955. What followed was a succession of stunning accomplishments. The NAUTILUS would reach the North Pole on 3 August 1958 during her 2,114-mile transit under the Polar Ice Cap. USS SKATE (SSN-578) would surface at the North Pole on 17 March 1959, demonstrating that submarines could operate year-round in the Arctic region. USS TRITON (SSN-586) would retrace Magellan's route to circumnavigate the globe in the 84 days between February and May of 1960.

One tragic event during the development of the nuclear submarine program was the loss of USS THRESHER (SSN-593) in 1963 off the coast of Nantucket. Investigators concluded that the cause of the accident was due to massive flooding in the engineering spaces which prevented the submarine from surfacing. As a result of this loss, the Sub Safe program was instituted and the deep submergence rescue vehicle (DSRV) was developed. The DSRV is a small submarine designed to "mate" with a submerged and disabled submarine, and rescue the crew.

The safety record of the nuclear propulsion plant is an undisputed triumph. In 1994, the U.S. Navy announced reaching 100 million accident-free miles of travel by its nuclear-powered fleet of submarines, cruisers, and aircraft carriers. The iron hand with which Admiral Rickover ruled his "nukes" was largely responsible for this exceptional safety record.

The buildup of the Cold War during the '60s resulted in designs for two new classes of U.S. Navy submarines:

USS HARTFORD (SSN-768) is launched in December of 1993. Built by General Dynamics Electric Boat Division, she's an Improved Los Angeles Class attack submarine (note the absence of dive planes on the sail). She was commissioned—delivered to the Navy—one year later, after successfully completing her sea trials. *US Navy*

the Los Angeles Class attack submarine (SSN–submersible ship, nuclear) and the Ohio Class ballistic missile submarine (SSBN–submersible ship, ballistic, nuclear). The attack submarine was designed to be faster, quieter, and more technologically advanced than her Russian counterpart. The ballistic missile submarine was designed to be a larger, quieter, and more sophisticated platform for the delivery of intercontinental ballistic missiles.

The Ohio Class submarine would prove to be virtually undetectable at sea. USS OHIO (SSBN-726) made the first operational patrol of its class in 1982. By June of 1992, 13 Ohio Class submarines were in operation. The 18th and final Ohio Class submarine, USS LOUISIANA (SSBN-743), was launched on July 27, 1996.

These warships would become key elements in America's deterrence and defense strategy known then as Mutually Assured Destruction (MAD). America's stick would be so big, no one would dare threaten our nation or our nation's interests abroad. These two classes today comprise America's modern submarine fleet and will serve us into the 21st century.

Twenty years have passed, however, since USS LOS ANGELES (SSN-688) was commissioned as the lead ship in a class of 62. The most modern U.S. Navy submarine, USS SEAWOLF (SSN-21), was launched in the summer of 1996. Two additional boats in this class of three have been approved. The long-term future of the U.S. Navy submarine program rests, however, in a yet-to-be-built warship—the new attack submarine, or NSSN.

What is the future of the U.S. submarine force now that the Cold War is over? Do we still need sub-marines? If we need them, how many are necessary, what will they do, and how shall we build them? These questions have been on the minds of our congressional representatives, our military leaders, members of the shipbuilding industry, and submariners worldwide, since the Cold War ended at the beginning of this decade.

Some of these questions have been addressed in an official paper known to all Navy personnel as *"Forward . . . From the Sea."* This document, drafted in 1994, describes a post-Cold War shift in the operational focus of the naval service. No longer will our naval forces be dealing with a single, global threat. Instead, we will be following regional conflicts, able to "project power and influence across the seas." Our battle groups will be "engaged in forward areas with the objectives of preventing conflicts and controlling crises." Most of this will take place in the shallow waters (the littoral) of coastal nations throughout the world.

More than 44 countries—including China, Iran, North Korea, Libya, Serbia, and Syria—operate over 600 submarines worldwide. Russia's new multi-mission submarine, the SEVERODVINSK, is expected to be operational by the year 2000. Some report it will outperform most advanced Western submarines.

The United States must stay on the cutting edge of technology, train smarter, do more with less, and do better with less. The shipbuilders have a mandate to build smaller but fully capable, multi-mission submarines; to build them using the most advanced design and construction methods; to build them faster, and at a lower cost.

We're not the only ones out there.

# ● ONE ●

# FAST ATTACK SUBMARINES:
## *Los Angeles Class (SSN-688)*

It's a predictably glorious December afternoon in San Diego, California—clear skies, bright sunshine, and a stiff, cold breeze coming across the bay from the Pacific Ocean. Guests are seated beneath a white tent set upon the pier. Draped with festive bunting, pennants, and medals, the black sail of a submarine is visible. A stage has been erected upon the deck of a Los Angeles Class attack submarine for the occasion of a change of command. A Navy band is playing as the last of the guests are seated.

We're here to witness a transfer of power. A new commanding officer is stepping forward to accept what has been referred to as "the unmatched burden of isolation"—command of a U.S. Navy submarine. He alone will be accountable for all that happens aboard

*"Submarines are an integral part of U.S. global influence and presence. Their stealth and endurance provide the Unified Commander enormous capabilities across the full spectrum of conflict."*
*General John M. Shalikashvili*
*Chairman, Joint Chiefs of Staff*

this ship and to her crew, in port as well as at sea. Although this submarine is in his command, he knows that the success or failure of the mission rests ultimately in the hands of over one hundred young men looking to him and to his officers for leadership, guidance, and knowledge.

"This is a warship," begins Captain Thomas L. Travis, then Commander of Submarine Squadron Eleven, "with the terrifying power to destroy ships and people." Captain Travis describes members of her crew as warriors who risk their lives. "They set and maintain the highest standards to ensure their return from sea."

The Los Angeles Class attack submarine is the U.S. Navy's most modern design presently on active

USS PITTSBURGH (SSN-720) was commissioned in November of 1985. The tubular bulge along the starboard side of the hull is the protective shroud for a towed array sonar system. This passive system (which listens for sounds, but does not emit them) relies on 2,600 feet of cable payed out and towed behind a submerged submarine underway. Hydrophones on the end of the cable pick up sounds that are then deciphered by Sonar Technicians in the Sonar room aboard the submarine. *US Navy*

A Chief Petty Officer stands at attention during a change of command ceremony. He, along with his fellow Chief Petty Officers, is wearing his Dolphin device above the left pocket.

duty in large numbers throughout the world. (When a new submarine design is approved and funded, the name of the very first ship built to these specifications is used to identify its "class.") USS LOS ANGELES (SSN-688) was the first of 62 submarines built to these basic specifications.

It was Admiral Hyman G. Rickover who determined and ordained that this class of submarine should and would become a reality. Rickover had tremendous power, partially due to his support by Congress whose members approved funding for this new class of submarine. The first 12 subs were named for the hometowns from which the supportive congressmen hailed, thereby setting a precedent for naming all subsequent boats of this class after U.S. cities.

The Los Angeles Class submarine was designed to be fast, quiet, and carry a payload of missiles and torpedoes with which to attack, subdue, or destroy an uncooperative adversary, whether surface ship or submarine. Attack submarines follow the noise they hear in the ocean—"prosecute the target." They're the bloodhounds, the police dogs.

The Los Angeles Class submarines were built in "flights" or groups, each one a little more sophisticated than the last. The first group (Flight I) of 24 submarines offered the most advanced and capable submersible ship designed for the U.S. fleet. USS LOS ANGELES (SSN-688) was commissioned in 1976, her design and construction based on technology of the late sixties.

Flight II boats incorporated important improvements into the initial design. First, a 12-tube vertical launch system (VLS) was added to the forward section of the boat to accommodate the Tomahawk and Harpoon missiles. The submarines were also coated with anechoic (free from echoes or reverberations)/ decoupling coating. This is a special surface that minimizes the effects of active pinging from another warship and reduces greatly the noises radiated from the submarine. Flight II submarines are equipped with a more powerful reactor (S6G) to compensate for the

USS KEY WEST (SSN-722) and USS SALT LAKE CITY (SSN-716) are moored side by side at Naval Submarine Base, San Diego, California. Both submarines are Flight I 688s and do not have the tell-tale 12-tube VLS doors on the bow. Each submarine is 360 feet in length with a draft of 32 feet and a beam of 33 feet.

| | |
|---|---|
| Displacement: | 6,900 tons submerged |
| Length: | 360 feet |
| Beam: | 33 feet |
| Draft: | 32 feet |
| Speed: | in excess of 25 knots |
| Depth: | in excess of 800 feet |
| Power Plant: | One nuclear reactor, two geared turbines, one shaft, approximately 35,000 shaft horsepower |
| Armament: | Harpoon and Tomahawk missiles (VLS) Mk48 & MK48 ADCAP torpedoes (four torpedo tubes) |
| Crew: | 129 (13 officers, 116 enlisted) |
| Flight 1: | First design (SSNs 688-718) |
| Flight 2: | Improvements: (SSNs 719-750)<br>• VLS<br>• more powerful reactor core |
| Flight 3: | Improved Los Angeles Class (688I)– (SSNs 751-773)<br>• Flight 2 improvements, plus:<br>• AN/BSY-1<br>• bow planes (instead of sail planes)<br>• improved quieting<br>• under-ice capability |

USS TUCSON (SSN-770) glides to the dock with the help of two tugboats, whose jets can move the tug in any direction. Bringing the submarine up to the dock is a critical maneuver made to look simple by proficient crews and support workers.

In the Control Center of USS JEFFERSON CITY (SSN-759), Commander W. "Marty" Smith (second from left with hands clasped) surveys the activities. Commander Smith has a BS in Chemical Engineering and a master's degree in Environmental Engineering. In early September 1996, the JEFFERSON CITY participated in a cruise missile strike against Iraq under Operation Desert Strike.

Underway in the forward port section of the Control Center aboard USS JEFFERSON CITY (SSN-759). The two young sailors in dungarees are driving the boat. The one to the rear is the planesman—he controls the movement of the dive planes. The one in the foreground is the helmsman—he controls the movement of the rudder. The man behind them dressed in khaki is the COB who monitors their every move in accordance with a precise sequence of commands and acknowledgments.

increased drag caused by the addition of the anechoic/decoupling coating.

It's the Flight III submarines, however, that carry the title "Improved Los Angeles Class." Sometimes a submariner will refer to a "Flight III 688" or 688I. We know he's talking about the Improved class. These boats, beginning with USS SAN JUAN (SSN-751), have not only the new reactor and VLS, but the following improvements or changes: bow planes instead of sail planes; additional quieting improvements; under-ice capabilities, including a reinforced fairwater (sail); and the AN/BSY-1 combat system. The last submarine of this class, USS COLUMBIA (SSN-771), was launched on September 24, 1994.

The BSY-1 (pronounced "busy-one") is important to the computer operations onboard the submarine. This piece of computer technology, known as distributed process architecture, links together the fire control, sensor, and weapons systems. Instead of having one huge main frame computer running all the systems, the BSY-1 acts as the lead processor, delegating assigned tasks to other computers that run specific processes (sonar, targeting). As a result, all systems run faster and are easier to upgrade.

Since adequate funding is not available to replace all 688 class submarines with new submarines featuring improved capabilities, modernizing the 688 is one of the submarine Navy's highest priorities. According to Rear Adm. E.P. Giambastiani, Director, Submarine Warfare Division, the submarine force must not only do more with less, but do better with less. And this means using state-of-the-art technology.

Transiting the surface, two playful dolphins try to outrun USS JEFFERSON CITY (SSN-759). Coordinates are written in grease pen on the plexiglass windscreen. A simple, off-the-shelf, marine radar device scans for surface traffic and is monitored below in the Control Center. The man on the left wears a red body harness to secure him to a railing on the top of the sail when he stands to survey the area with binoculars.

USS HOUSTON (SSN-713) prepares to depart. The tug is getting into position; line handlers are at parade rest on deck wearing life vests; and the hatch just aft of the sail is open. A diver is stationed on the aft of the submarine.

In 1998, the U.S. Navy will begin a $300 million program to modernize each 688 expected to be on active duty beyond the year 2000. These improvements will be in the areas of communications (Extremely High Frequency satellite links and use of the Global Broadcasting System), acoustic data processing, sensors, and weapons. Changes to the software of the Mk48 ADCAP torpedo will allow it to operate more effectively in shallow, coastal waters. In addition, much of the submarine's proprietary data processing equipment will be replaced with commercially available processors that are more advanced, cheaper, and easier to upgrade.

Fast attack submarines perform seven traditional missions: peacetime engagement; surveillance and intelligence; special operations; precision strikes; sea denial; deterrence; and sea control. Most submariners believe that the full potential of the submarine has yet to be realized and that other missions will be carried out in the future.

Peacetime Engagement: During peacetime, attack submarines can be highly visible indications of America's national interest in any region, worldwide. In 1991, U.S. submarines conducted more than 200 port visits to 50 cities around the world. We let it be known that we can navigate the planet at will, either visible or invisible.

Surveillance and Intelligence: Submarines have always been used for surveillance, information gathering, and warning. Because they're stealthy, submarines can secretly enter an area and collect information. The use of the submarine as an intelligence gathering plat-

Protective devices cover missiles stored in the torpedo room aboard a submarine. Notice in the left edge of the frame the tangle of wires, pipes, and valves that line the hull in the background. All systems are exposed for quick and easy access.

MARK 48 Torpedo

| | |
|---|---|
| Length: | 19 feet |
| Diameter: | 21 inches |
| Weight: | 3,520 pounds |
| Maximum speed: | 55 knots |
| Power Plant: | Piston engine; pump jet |
| Maximum Range: | 23 miles |
| Maximum Depth: | 500 fathoms |
| Warhead: | 650 pounds of high explosives |
| Contractors: | Hughes, Westinghouse |

MARK 48 ADCAP (Advanced Capability)

This replacement for the Mark 48 is being delivered to the fleet and will be aboard all classes of attack submarines. The ADCAP offers more speed and accuracy than any other torpedo in the Navy's history. The ADCAP's digitally based guidance system, which enables the torpedo to operate effectively in severe acoustic conditions (shallow coastal waters), is the major upgrade over the Mark 48. Trident submarines still use the Mark 48, not the ADCAP, because of differences in fire control capabilities.

RIGHT: Pacific Ocean . . . A Tomahawk cruise missile is launched from the nuclear-powered attack submarine USS LA JOLLA (SSN-701) on the Pacific Missile Test Center (PMTC) range. *US Navy / Gerry Winey*

form was a vital factor in winning the Cold War and this mission will always be vital to our nation's defense. To ever improve this capability, testing and evaluation of unmanned aerial vehicles and unmanned undersea vehicles controlled from the submarine has begun.

In early June of 1996, USS CHICAGO (SSN-721) controlled an unmanned aerial vehicle—Predator UAV—for 26 hours out to a range of 104 miles in a special exercise off the coast of Southern California. The idea was to use the UAV to survey from above the selected target—in this scenario, a missile site. Using the Predator's video downlink, U.S. Navy SEALs were deployed and directed to the target. They could then monitor the site and support a precision aircraft strike. During this operation, the submarine controlled the UAV, known now as "the world's tallest periscope." In addition, the Navy is developing a self-propelled unmanned undersea vehicle that can be launched and

recovered from a torpedo tube. The vehicle will be guided by fiber optics and provide real time displays back to the submarine.

Special Operations: Submarines have long been used for carrying commandos, reconnaissance teams,

# NUCLEAR PROPULSION

The propulsion plant of a nuclear-powered ship is based upon use of a nuclear reactor to provide heat. The heat comes from the fissioning of nuclear fuel contained within the reactor. When the reactor is operating, it is said to be "running critical." Since the fissioning process also produces radiation, shields are placed around the reactor so that the crew is protected. The nuclear propulsion plant in U.S. Navy submarines uses a pressurized water reactor design that has two basic systems: the primary system and the secondary system.

The primary system circulates ordinary water and consists of the reactor, piping loops, pumps, and steam generators. The heat produced in the reactor is transferred to the water under high pressure so it does not boil. The water is pumped through the steam generators and back into the reactor for reheating. In the steam generators, the heat from the water in the primary system is transferred to the secondary system to create steam.

The secondary system is isolated from the primary system so that the water in the two systems does not intermix. In the secondary system, the steam flows from the steam generators to drive the turbine generators, which supply the ship with electricity, and to the main propulsion turbines, which drive the propeller. After passing through the turbines, the steam is condensed into water which is fed back to the steam generators by the feed pumps.

Thus, both the primary and secondary systems are closed systems where water is recirculated and reused. There is no step in the generation of this power which requires the presence of air or oxygen. This allows the ship to operate completely independent from the earth's atmosphere for extended periods of time.

*US Navy*

A warning placard hanging from a loaded torpedo tube aboard a Los Angeles Class attack submarine reminds everyone of the true nature and real purpose of a submarine. Los Angeles Class attack submarines carry Mk48 and Mk48 ADCAP (Advanced Capability) torpedoes as offensive and defensive weapons.

and agents on high-risk missions. Most special operations by submarines are carried out by teams of U.S. Navy SEALs.

Precision Strikes: U.S. attack submarines carry the Tomahawk Land Attack Missile (TLAM), which provides the capability for long-range, precision strikes with conventional warheads against shore targets. During the Gulf War, U.S. surface ships and submarines fired land-attack

Work never stops for the crews of a submarine. Moored alongside the submarine tender USS McKee (AS-41), workers on the deck of USS LA JOLLA (SSN-701) work into the night under banks of bright lights.

variants of the Tomahawk missile. USS LOUISVILLE (SSN-724), operating in the Red Sea, launched eight missiles, and USS PITTSBURGH (SSN-720) launched four TLAMs from the eastern Mediterranean.

In early September 1996, USS JEFFERSON CITY (SSN-759) participated in a cruise missile strike against selected air defense targets in Iraq under Operation Desert Strike. This improved Los Angeles Class submarine was operating as part of the Maritime interception force under the U.S. Fifth Fleet.

Sea Denial: Stopping enemy surface ships and submarines from using the seas is an important mission for submarines. This may take place at strategic "choke points," along sea lanes, or in enemy ports. The goal is to destroy enemy surface ships, merchant vessels, and

It's not uncommon to see this much scaffolding on a submarine. Work is always being done while in port. The specially contoured platform for the torpedo load is also lowered by crane into position.

LEFT: With the aid of a bright yellow crane stationed on the dock, a torpedo is swung from the dock. Men on the deck of the submarine guide the torpedo with ropes toward the submarine. The string of bright orange buoys floating on the water around the submarine is designed to contain any accidental spills of contaminants during routine overhaul and maintenance work.

submarines. The weapon of choice for this mission is the Mk48 torpedo. Submarines also carry mines to deny sea areas to enemy surface ships or submarines. Harbors or narrow sea passages leading to strategic locations are prime locations for planting these devices.

Deterrence: Strategic deterrence remains a fundamental element of U.S. defense strategy. Although the presence of an attack submarine would be, for most, a

RIGHT: The loading tray is raised up to allow the torpedo to be lowered into the submarine. Another group of men down below will go through a series of maneuvers to align the torpedo properly in the torpedo room.

sufficient deterrent against war and aggression, deterrence remains the supreme mission of the Ohio Class nuclear ballistic missile submarines.

Sea Control: keeping the sea lanes open—remains essential to our national security and is still the primary mission of U.S. Navy submarines.

Los Angeles Class attack submarines are based in the Atlantic (Groton, Connecticut, and Norfolk, Virginia) and in the Pacific (Pearl Harbor, Hawaii, and San Diego, California). From these ports, Los Angeles Class submarines deploy year-round on 6-month patrols throughout the world, either as part of a carrier battle group or on independent operations. U.S. nuclear-powered submarines are capable of navigating the earth's five oceans—over 141,000 square miles—covering 70 percent of the earth's surface. Los Angeles Class submarines visit friendly, foreign ports and U.S. naval installations abroad. During these short visits, crew members phone loved ones at home, breathe some fresh air, and take on more food and supplies.

The torpedo is being lowered onto a cradle-like loading tray which can then be repositioned to allow the torpedo to be angled down into the submarine. The man wearing the red hardhat is holding an open procedure manual and appears to be monitoring each step in this important sequence. The Weapons Officer supervises this activity.

Two tugboats back USS HOUSTON (SSN-713) out into the bay and point her toward the open mouth of the harbor. Divers in black wetsuits are fore and aft. The small gray lifeguard boat will trail the submarine out of the harbor, just in case someone falls overboard. Hull numbers are removed when a submarine goes to sea.

A VLS (Vertical Launch System) tube is being lowered by dockside crane into USS CHICAGO (SSN-721). Flight II and Flight III 688s are equipped with the VLS.

USS PASADENA (SSN-752) is an improved Los Angeles Class attack submarine. Her dive planes are located on the bow, not on the sail. The white markings on the deck aft of the sail indicate a docking location for a DSRV (Deep Submergence Rescue Vehicle). *US Navy*

# ━ TWO ━

# BALLISTIC MISSILE SUBMARINES
## Ohio Class (SSBN-726)

The Ohio Class ballistic missile submarines, also known as "boomers" or Tridents, after the type of missile they carry, are the largest to be built in the United States (only the six Typhoon Class submarines built by the Russians are larger). Tridents measure 560 feet in length and displace 18,700 tons of seawater. When you look at a photograph of a Trident submarine transiting the surface, you see only 17 percent of the boat—the other 83 percent remains underwater. Crew members love them because there's so much room inside. The rest of us are simply in awe of their size and destructive power. They are awesome warships. They are the Navy's nuclear deterrent force; their job is to strike with their nuclear missiles if ordered by the President; their torpedoes are used for defense.

> "However warm our relationship might grow with the new former Soviet Republics; however close our relationships become—we will always, always place our faith in our boomers and not in anyone else."
>
> *General Colin Powell, US Army Chairman of the Joint Chiefs of Staff, April 1992*

The reason to have such a large submarine is to carry an immense payload—in this case, missiles . . . big missiles . . . lots of missiles. Each Trident I (C4) missile is 34 feet long, 6 feet in diameter, weighs 71,000 pounds, and costs around $13 million. The Trident II (D5) missile is even bigger (see sidebar) and is carried on Ohio Class submarines operating out of King's Bay, Georgia. There are 24 missile tubes on each Ohio Class submarine. They stand patiently at attention in two neat rows aft of the sail, cutting through all levels of the submarine interior.

Once launched, a Trident I missile can travel 4,000 nautical miles to reach a predetermined target on enemy shore. The United States has other methods of delivering destructive power—from land-based launch sites or from aircraft—but the Ohio Class sub-

---

USS MAINE (SSBN-741) during seal trials (1994/1995). The tear-drop shapes on the top of the sail are the tops of various masts, antennae, and periscopes, fully retracted at the time of this photo. *General Dynamics, Electric Boat Division*

We're in the missile compartment—also known as "Sherwood Forest"—aboard USS OHIO (SSBN-726) standing between missile tubes #23 and #24. Each Trident 1/C4 missile is 34 feet long and over 6 feet in diameter. The tubes cut vertically through all levels of the submarine. Missile tubes are painted to give better depth perception to crew members walking through the missile compartment : the first 8 are one color, the next group of 8 is a little darker, and the last group of 8 is even darker. Pipes and cables run overhead. Stationed throughout the missile compartment is firefighting equipment and other safety devices.  The passageway floor is clean and waxed.

marine is more survivable than other legs of the system. It can cruise undetected in the depths of the ocean, out of harm's way, and launch missiles while submerged. The function of an Ohio Class submarine is to transport and care for its missiles, deterring all would-be aggressors with the horrific nature of her mission. It's estimated that one modern warhead contains more firepower than what was unleashed on Hiroshima and Nagasaki combined.

Trident missiles are cared for as if they were exotic birds. Safely nestled in their individual tubes, they're pampered around the clock. Two MTs (Missile Technicians) stand watch in the missile compartment. One of them patrols on foot all four levels of the huge compartment. The rover watches for fire hazards and sea leaks, checks to make sure all security access doors are shut, and reports back to his partner every 30 minutes that all indications are normal.

The partner, meanwhile, stands by the Control and Monitoring Panel (CAMP). He monitors each missile tube for temperature, humidity, air, pneumatics, hydraulics, and pressure. Warm or cool water is routed through a system of pipes within the tube to maintain a specific temperature. If it gets too humid in the tube, warm dry air is blown into the tube to reduce the humidity. MTs selected for this assignment must be reliable and trustworthy and are screened carefully for this important duty.

Two 4-man teams of Missile Technicians perform maintenance inside the missile itself and participate in the critical launch sequence. In the event of a launch, one team is in charge of the twelve missiles in the forward section of the missile compartment, and the other team is in charge of the twelve missiles in the aft section of the missile compartment.

The missile contains electronics packages, components, and guidance systems that require periodic testing and maintenance. If it's necessary to replace a component, the team gets permission from the Commanding Officer, through the Weapons Officer on board, and proceeds with the maintenance.

Missile Control Center aboard USS OHIO (SSBN-726). The MT (Missile Technician) on the left monitors the Fire Control console and the MT on the right monitors the Launcher console. The Weapons Officer oversees the activities of these MTs. Interface with Navigation and Sonar is necessary to launch a weapon.

This is the CAMP (Control and Monitoring Panel). A Petty Officer is stationed here to monitor the physical conditions in the missile tubes—temperature, humidity. His partner roves the missile compartment on foot as security guard and must report back to his buddy at the panel every 30 minutes.

No Trident missiles have been fired in anger against an enemy. Practice exercises are conducted periodically to make sure crew members are ready for action and that the missiles perform according to specs. It must be a thrill for the crew to launch one of these weapons in a practice exercise. Here's what happens.

It's not as easy as pulling the trigger. Permission to launch is handed down to the captain from shore-based command and control. During wartime, instructions come via encrypted messages which must be authenticated by officers on board following strict procedures. It takes teams of people manning sophisticated computer systems to launch a missile.

In order to fire a missile, the ship's position must be known. The submarine's position is determined using GPS (global positioning system). Another system, SINS (ship's inertial navigational system), tracks the submarine's position from this known starting point, as well as from periodic GPS updates while at sea. Navigation's mission is to support Fire Control in the Missile Control Center by giving an accurate position.

The term Fire Control has nothing to do with fighting fires aboard ship; it refers to the firing of a missile or torpedo. The Missile Control Center features two major systems: Fire Control (the brains) and Launcher (the brawn). Fire Control takes the information from Navigation, interfaces with the computer systems within each missile, and assigns target information. Fire Control monitors the launch sequence and sends targeting information to the missiles, selecting a specific missile, and telling it where to go. It's a very exact science.

While the MT (Missile Technician) at the Fire Control Console is proceeding with the countdown, the MT at the Launcher Console is monitoring the missiles to ensure that temperature and humidity within the tubes are at optimum, that they are pressurized correctly, and that the hydraulic systems are functioning properly—the hatch on one of these missile tubes weighs 8 tons and snaps open in 2 seconds.

To launch a missile, the submarine hovers at launch depth, dead in the water. The interior of the missile tube is pressurized with nitrogen to equal that of the surrounding sea, so that when the hatch opens, the sea pressure will not crush the fiberglass closure device covering the "nose" of the missile. Deep in the missile tube a canister of water with a little rocket on top of it makes a huge volume of steam at the bottom of the tube, pushing the missile out like a pea from a peashooter.

When the missile is fired, a detonator cord embedded in the fiberglass closure device receives an electrical charge, causing the closure device to burst.

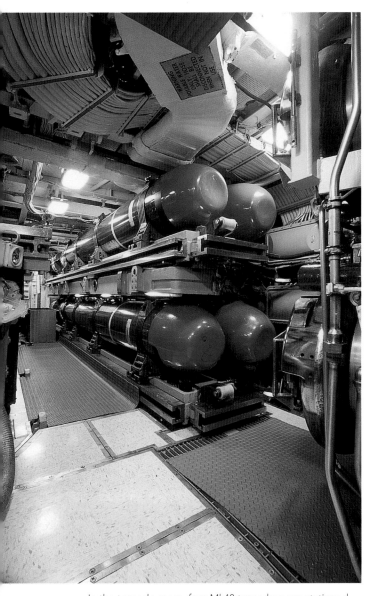

In the torpedo room, four Mk48 torpedoes are stationed for loading. The racks supporting the torpedoes can be moved within the torpedo room, depending on which tubes (port or starboard) are to be loaded. It takes teamwork and good communication to rapidly load and reload these weapons.

RIGHT: Two torpedo tubes are stacked vertically on each side of the sub. Both of these portside tubes are already loaded. The network of tubes, pipes, and valves attests to the power and complexity of the system. Torpedomen know how everything in here works. Note how the floor panels can be unscrewed and removed.

The nitrogen bubble comes up, pushing the fiberglass pieces of the closure device out of the way, and the missile and the rest of the nitrogen bubble rise at the same rate—the missile never gets wet. A shudder ripples throughout the ship creating pressure on the hull for about 30 seconds. As the missile clears the deck and breaks the surface of the ocean, it will begin to decelerate. At this moment, sensors ignite the solid rocket engine, and off it goes into the sky, leaving the submarine behind. The computer program on board the missile takes over from here, guiding the missile to its destination, while the submarine disappears into the depths of the sea.

The submariners are businesslike and deliberate throughout the launch sequence. Adrenaline flows freely and a sense of excitement is in the air, but everything is by the book. A debriefing and overall evaluation takes place after the launch, since everything on board a submarine is a training exercise to hone skills and ensure readiness for the real thing.

All Ohio Class ballistic missile submarines were built by General Dynamics Electric Boat Division, including the 18th and final of its class, USS LOUISIANA (SSBN-743) launched on July 27, 1996. All are powered by a General Electric S8G pressurized water-cooled nuclear reactor that produces over 60,000 shaft horsepower. The reactor makes steam for Westinghouse geared turbines that drive the screw.

The hull was built using modular construction. Separate cylinders, 42 feet in diameter, are welded together to form a long, cylindrical submarine. Modular construction, coupled with even more advanced computer technology, is expected to greatly reduce the construction time for future classes of submarines, thereby reducing the cost.

The Trident Refit Facility, Bangor, Washington. The hot test bed area of Bldg. 7000 is where periscopes for Pacific Fleet Tridents are tested, repaired, and certified. The type 8J found on Tridents is 48 feet in length, 7.5 inches in diameter, and weighs just under 2,000 lbs. They're hermetically sealed against gas, air, and water. Periscopes receive an optical and a mechanical inspection whenever the sub returns from patrol. If the periscope needs repair, it's brought to the Refit Facility. These periscopes are reliable and may need repair only once every 2-5 years.

Looking toward the front of USS NEVADA (SSBN-733), three of the twenty-four Trident missile doors are open. Each door weighs 8 tons and snaps open in 2 seconds. Visible in the foreground are two blue protective casings on the "business end" of each missile. *Hans Halberstadt*

All Ohio Class submarines receive their orders from USSTRATCOM (U.S. Strategic Command) located at Offutt Air Force Base in Nebraska. Two U.S. naval bases support Ohio Class submarines: Bangor, Washington, and King's Bay, Georgia. Both bases are multi-billion dollar complexes designed to support the Ohio Class submarines, her crew, and the hundreds of entities needed to sustain a successful, ongoing mission. Each has a Trident Training Facility and a Trident Refit Facility. Submarines in Bangor are fitted with the Trident I/C4 missile. Those in King's Bay carry the more advanced Trident II/D5.

Each base has a Strategic Weapons Facility responsible for assembling, storing, loading, and transporting the missiles. The Strategic Weapons Facility is guarded around the clock by U.S. Marines patrolling in vehicles and on foot with guns and dogs. The area is clear-cut (for high visibility and to reduce the threat of fire), surrounded with barbed wire fences, and equipped with motion sensors. Lockheed, in conjunction with hundreds of subcontractors, builds about 95 percent of the missile. The remaining 5 percent, or "business end" of the missile, is built by the Navy. The missiles are transported by truck or by rail to the Explosives Handling Wharf. Here the missiles are loaded onto the submarines by civilians employed by the Navy. Weapons are actually leased from the contractor and are not purchased until the Navy fires them—an arrangement known informally as "you fly 'em; you buy 'em."

Unlike Los Angeles Class fast attack submarines that surface periodically in foreign ports, ballistic missile submarines remain invisible throughout their 75-day sea patrol. They don't surface in foreign ports, and only rarely transmit radio messages. They listen. The Radio

This submariner has the topside watch on USS ALASKA (SSBN-732) in drydock behind him. He's armed with a 12-gauge shotgun, carries a 45 caliber weapon on his waist, and has a portable radio. He's wearing dungarees that feature a set of Dolphins embroidered above his left pocket.

USS NEVADA (SSBN-733) submerging in Dabob Bay near Naval Submarine Base, Bangor. When the main ballast tanks are open, water floods in, forcing air out of the tanks through vents on top. *Hans Halberstadt*

The deck of the NEVADA is submerged leaving only the sail visible. As a safety precaution, the dive planes are angled up and down to test the hydraulic systems before submerging the submarine. *Hans Halberstadt*

The periscopes of the NEVADA are all that's left (visible) of an 18,000-ton submarine. This is probably a common sight for the folks who live ashore along the waters near the submarine base. *Hans Halberstadt*

USS ALASKA (SSBN-732) in drydock at Naval Submarine Base, Bangor, Washington. The drydock is about 62 feet deep. Seawater has already been pumped out and routed to a water treatment plant ashore before going back into the Hood Canal. The submarine is positioned off center for two reasons: (1) to allow large pieces of machinery to move around safely on one side of the sub, and (2) to accommodate the limited length of the brow—the footbridge from the dock to the deck of the submarine. The two rectangular patches on the port side of the hull just above the two scaffolding units are the torpedo tube doors. The vents on the underside of the hull above the worker's head exchange seawater in and out of the forward main ballast tanks.

Room is a classified area adjacent to the Control Center where specialists decode encrypted messages originating from USSTRATCOM. The Trident's mission is to remain stealthy—undetected—at all times. They do not "chase" other targets. They fire torpedoes in defensive situations only. As one submariner described it, "The 688s go after the noise; the "boomers" run away from the noise."

The Control Center is the focal point for what goes on aboard all submarines. The Control Center is located on Level 1 just below the sail. Look for two periscopes on a raised platform, and you'll know you're in the Control Center. Here, up to 28 officers and men can work side-by-side to monitor and control key aspects of the submarine's activities and

This is the underside of the ALASKA in drydock. Visible are the huge vents that allow movement of seawater in and out of the ballast tanks. The hull rests on a system of cement blocks lined with Sitka spruce cut to the shape of the hull. Each time a submarine goes into drydock, the resting position is changed slightly to avoid creating weak spots.

movement while at sea—navigation, direction and depth control, radio communication, and fire control. Two plotting tables in the Control Center are used by quartermasters who continuously monitor the ship's position while at sea. They provide navigational data to the Officer of the Deck to support the safe navigation of the submarine.

# MISSILES

### Trident I (C4) Missile

| | |
|---|---|
| Length: | 34 feet |
| Diameter: | 6 feet, 2 inches |
| Weight: | 70,000 pounds |
| Range: | 4,000 nautical miles |
| Power plant: | 3-stage solid fuel rocket, with inertial guidance |
| Warheads: | thermonuclear heads: <br> • MIRV (Multiple Independently targetable Re-entry Vehicle) <br> • MARV (Maneuverable Re-entry Vehicle) |
| Contractor: | Lockheed |

### Trident II (D5) Missile

| | |
|---|---|
| Length: | 44 feet |
| Diameter: | 83 inches |
| Weight: | approximately 126,000 pounds |
| Range: | 6,000 nautical miles |
| Power Plant: | 3-stage solid-propellant rocket, with inertial guidance |
| Warheads: | thermonuclear heads: <br> • MIRV (Multiple Independently targetable Re-entry Vehicle) <br> • MARV (Maneuverable Re-entry Vehicle) |
| Contractor: | Lockheed |

### Harpoon Missile

| | |
|---|---|
| Weight: | 1,530 lbs. |
| Length: | 15 feet |
| Diameter: | 13 inches |
| Speed: | Mach 0.85 |
| Range: | 75-80 nautical miles |
| Guidance: | Active radar |
| Propulsion: | Turbojet, plus solid-propellant booster |
| Warhead: | 510 lbs. high explosive |

### Tomahawk Missile

| | |
|---|---|
| Length: | 18 feet (plus 2-ft. booster) |
| Diameter: | 21 inches |
| Speed: | 550 mph, approx. |
| Weight: | 2,650 lbs. (plus 550-lb. booster, plus 1,000-lb capsule for submarine underwater launch) |
| Propulsion: | Turbofan, plus solid-propellant booster |
| Range: | TLAM, 700 nautical miles |

The planesman on the left controls the movements of the dive planes on the sail of USS OHIO (SSBN-726). The helmsman on the right controls movement of the tail rudder. These young seamen are closely supervised by senior personnel who stand behind them. Various dials and gauges are covered in this photo for security reasons.

The Navigation Center is also on Level 1, slightly aft of the Control Center. In a normal watch station, two ETs (Electronics Technicians) man the area. Navigation, operation, and sonar programs are maintained in the Nav Center, which supports the missiles on board. The D5 Nav Center supports the Trident II/D5 missile, found on Ohio Class submarines based at King's Bay. They feature UNIX workstations, CD-ROM, and beryllium ball gyros.

The drive functions (diving, surfacing, turning) are manned by a planesman and a helmsman, often the youngest and least experienced members of the crew—average age, 22 years. They're supervised closely by other senior crew members who stand behind them, giving commands and monitoring their handling of the controls. Also found in this area are panels of instruments by which to control ballast in the main ballast tanks.

Here in the Control Center are the Fire Control work stations. Fire Control Technicians (FTs) specialize in the operation of the ship's tactical weapons control system. They are responsible for ensuring that the tactical weapons systems are ready to fire at a moment's notice.

USS FLORIDA (SSBN-728). The footbridge from the dock to the deck bearing the ship's name and hull number is called the brow. It's raised and lowered into position by dockside crane. While in port, each of the three hatch openings is protected by a variety of coverings, from little tents to actual cabin-like structures. A temporary safety railing is visible on the bow. The capstans (cleats onto which the lines are tied) are retracted when underway.

| | |
|---|---|
| Displacement: | 18,700 tons submerged |
| Length: | 560 feet |
| Beam: | 42 feet |
| Draft: | 36 feet |
| Speed: | 25+ knots submerged |
| Depth: | Greater than 800 feet |
| Power Plant: | One nuclear reactor, two geared turbines, one shaft, approximately 60,000 horsepower |
| Armament: | Missiles (24-tube capacity): Trident I (C4): SSBN 726-733 Trident II (D5): SSBN 734-743 Torpedoes  MK48 (4-tube capacity): |
| Crew: | approx. 172 (16 officers plus 156 enlisted) |
| Builder: | General Dynamics, Electric Boat |

USS NEVADA (SSBN-733), clean and sleek.  The four small holes visible along the port side of the hull allow the deployment of explosive decoys.  The small protrusion on the bow contains a hydrophone. *Hans Halberstadt*

Fire Control's job is to calculate—using course, speed, range, bearing—the movement and location of a target in relation to the submarine's movement and location, and to plot a course for a torpedo launch. Fire Control gets this information from Sonar. Once a solution has been plotted, Fire Control can "tell" the torpedo when, where, and how to go.

Down in the torpedo room on Level 4, TMs (Torpedoman's Mates or Torpedomen) operate and maintain torpedo tubes and associated tube-launched weapons. They ensure proper operation of the torpedo tube system during combat operations, and supervise the movement and reloading of weapons into the torpedo tubes. During shore-based training, TMs practice the teamwork and communication skills necessary for the smooth, swift loading and reloading of torpedoes.

Ohio Class submarines use a turbine ejection pump to get the torpedo out of the submarine. High-pressure hydraulics squeeze the torpedo, "like pinching a water-

USS ALASKA (SSBN-732) waits patiently for buoyancy as water is pumped into the dry dock at Naval Submarine Base, Bangor, Washington.

melon seed between your fingers." Standing at his panel of buttons and switches, the TM "talks" to the torpedoes, routing information to them from Fire Control—entering "pre-sets" like when to turn, how many degrees, at what speed, etc. From this panel, the TM can flood the tube, open the doors, and fire the torpedo as instructed.

When the torpedo is fired, a wire pays out from both the shipboard coil and torpedo coil as these two vehicles (submarine and torpedo) move through the water. This leaves the payed out wire stationary with respect to the earth. A protective, hose-like sheath resembling an electrical conduit protects the wire from chaffing and possible breakage. Onboard systems are able to communicate additional or modified instructions to the torpedo guidance system through this wire.

The Mk48 torpedo is designed to explode beneath an enemy warship causing it to collapse into the void cre-

USS HENRY M. JACKSON (SSBN-730) is in refit at Delta Pier, Naval Submarine Base, Bangor. The gigantic cranes can move along the perimeter of the triangular-shaped dock by way of what look like very wide train tracks. The dive planes are being tested; here, they are pointing up as they would be during surfacing.

ated by the torpedo's explosion. The target ship will implode by virtue of its own weight and mass. A torpedo launch takes about 2 minutes; a "snapshot" (panic) launch, 45 seconds. Trident submarines utilize torpedoes primarily as defensive weapons, whereas attack submarines use them as both offensive and defensive weapons.

Transiting on the surface, in and out of port or in shipping lanes, is one of the most hazardous places for submarines, due to the risk of collision. The maneuvering watch begins with crew members on high alert for possible traffic. One or both periscopes are manned, someone below is monitoring a radar screen, sonar is listening for merchant traffic, and at least two members of the crew are topside with binoculars on the sail, in visual contact with any and all traffic within their 360-degree view. Radio is in communication with other vessels within range. The Officer of the Deck topside is in charge of the entire watch and is in phone communication with crew members below in the Control Center.

The transit through the Hood Canal and the Straits of Juan de Fuca from Naval Submarine Base Bangor to the Pacific is 155 miles long and takes about 8 hours. The Coast Guard controls these

A group of visitors have found a warm, dry place to take a nap–the bow of USS FLORIDA (SSBN-728). Naval Submarine Base, Bangor, employs a full-time game warden and biologist to oversee the base plant and wildlife population. The Hood Canal has an EPA rating of "pristine." *Official US Navy Photo*

An unidentified Ohio Class submarine leaves an enormous wake while transiting the surface. Without a hull number, there's no way to know which submarine is in view. The white markings fore and aft of the sail mark the locations of escape hatches to which a DSRV (Deep Submergence Rescue Vehicle) could dock. *General Dynamics, Electric Boat Division*

inland waters, and the general policy is for Tridents to transit on the surface to avoid accidents with other maritime traffic. Submarines are vulnerable on the surface, particularly if there's fog or bad weather. They are often difficult for merchant traffic to see, and their sails present only a small radar target. This explains the rare collision between submarines and merchant vessels in friendly waters offshore. Happy is the Captain who can finally submerge into the depths of the ocean, a submarine's true home.

Trident submarines have two separate, identical crews (referred to as "Blue" and "Gold") that alternate manning each Ohio Class submarine. While one crew takes the boat to sea on its regular cycle of refit and two-month patrol, the other crew is ashore enjoying R&R and refresher training in preparation for their next patrol. This enables maximum utilization of the submarine at sea, while giving some relief to crew members.

When a Trident submarine returns from patrol, both crews work together for a few days. The offgoing crew briefs the new crew on the status of the many systems on board. The incoming crew works extended hours getting ready for their next patrol. Components and systems needing repair are fixed. All systems are tested and evaluated according to an extensive checklist and set of procedures. Everything must be operating correctly and safely before the submarine departs on its next patrol.

Assignment to an Ohio Class submarine is considered the ultimate duty. The working spaces are large, habitability is outstanding (generally, there's no need to "hot bunk"), and time at sea out on patrol is relatively short (about 75-90 days).

**51**

# THREE

# SEAWOLF CLASS (SSN-21) AND NEW ATTACK SUBMARINE (NSSN)

On July 5, 1996, USS SEAWOLF (SSN-21), the nation's newest and most advanced submarine, returned to the Electric Boat (EB) shipyard in Groton, Connecticut, following the successful completion of its initial sea trials—a shakedown of the propulsion plant and the entire ship and equipment at full speed and at test depth. The Seawolf returned to the shipyard displaying a broom on her sail—a traditional naval signal that the alpha trials had been a "clean sweep," a success.

Admiral DeMars, Director Navy Nuclear Propulsion, participated in the sea trials and said upon his return, "This is a great day both for the Navy and for the nation. The ship behind us is the most complicated thing built in this country."

*"Let me tell you— she's a sweetheart."*
*Capt. (select) David McCall*
*Commanding Officer*
*USS SEAWOLF (SSN-21)*
*Return from Alpha Sea Trials, July 5, 1996*

The Seawolf is thought to be the quietest and most heavily armed submarine in the world. The Seawolf's flexibility gives the U.S. Navy an undersea weapons platform able to carry out its missions against any threat. Her primary improvements and advantages are in the areas of stealth (quietness), mobility (speed & depth), endurance (due to an increased weapons payload), and technology. In addition, the Seawolf has improved sensors which enable her to perform better by detecting enemy targets sooner and with more precision.

Because of her speed and quietness capabilities, the Seawolf can transport her crew and weapons to the far corners of the globe in a short amount of time, remaining undetected en route. The Seawolf can carry more weapons than a Los

Returning from her hugely successful Alpha Sea Trials in July of 1996, the crew of USS SEAWOLF (SSN-21) displays a broom on the sail—an old Navy tradition to indicate that the evolution was a "clean sweep." Note the sloping, forward edge of the sail where it joins the deck. *General Dynamics Electric Boat Division*

Angeles Class submarine, thus allowing her to remain longer on patrol.

The Seawolf is Arctic capable. Sophisticated onboard systems allow safer navigation under the ice, and a reinforced sail permits penetration through the ice. The Seawolf is designed to more easily accommodate onboard teams of U.S. Navy SEALs or other special forces units. Presently, only the Trident and Sturgeon class submarines can comfortably transport special forces teams. Quarters for teams are make-shift and cramped aboard a Los Angeles Class submarine, where special forces "pas-

USS SEAWOLF (SSN-21) under construction. The name Seawolf dates back to 1913, the year the diesel submarine, USS SEAWOLF (SS-28), was commissioned. Another Seawolf followed in 1957, USS SEAWOLF (SSN-575), the world's second nuclear powered submarine. *General Dynamics Electric Boat Division*

# SEAWOLF CLASS (SSN-21)

| | |
|---|---|
| Displacement: | 9,130 tons submerged |
| Length: | 353 feet |
| Beam: | 42 feet |
| Maximum Speed: | 25+ knots |
| Complement: | 133 |
| Weapons: | Tomahawk, Harpoon, and Mk 48 ADCAP Torpedoes launched from 8 tubes amidships |
| Radar: | AN/BPS-16 surface search |
| Sonar/Fire Control: | AN/BSY-2 with bow-mounted transducers and hull-mounted Wide Aperture Array TB-16 towed array TB-29 towed array |

Today's USS SEAWOLF (SSN-21) is the first in a class of three submarines. One obvious design element that distinguishes her visually from an Improved Los Angeles Class submarine is the filleted forward edge of the sail where it joins the deck. *General Dynamics Electric Boat Division*

The world's newest and most capable nuclear-powered attack submarine, USS SEAWOLF (SSN-21), was christened on June 24, 1995. *General Dynamics Electric Boat Division*

sengers" bunk out in the torpedo room. Stowage of their gear is also a problem. Beginning with the Seawolf, submarines will be designed to better accommodate special forces units.

The SSN-21 program began in 1982. Once a series of designs were completed, reviewed, and approved, the authorization for the production of a lead ship was granted in 1988. In 1991 the discovery of defects in the hull welds of the lead ship delayed the delivery schedule of SSN-21 approximately one year. The second submarine in the Seawolf Class—USS CONNECTICUT (SSN-22)—is under construction and expected to be

# NSSN: NEW ATTACK SUBMARINE

| | |
|---|---|
| Length: | 377 feet |
| Displacement: | 7,500 tons |
| Draft: | 32 feet |
| Speed: | 25+ knots |
| Test depth: | 800+ feet |
| Weapons: | Tomahawk and Harpoon missiles Mark 48 ADCAP Torpedo • 12 missiles in vertical launch tubes • 24 weapons in torpedo room • 4 torpedo tubes |
| Crew: | 134 |

completed sometime in 1998. Construction on SSN-23 (yet unnamed) began in December 1995.

Thirteen years is a lengthy production cycle for a weapons system that claims to be "cutting edge." The U.S. Navy has therefore made a commitment to better utilize current technology by waiving, in some circumstances, mandatory reliance on components built to military specifications. Instead, more widespread use of COTS, "commercial off the shelf," components is expected to reduce costs, improve upgrades, speed up production, and keep the military at the leading edge of available technology. Another factor improving productivity was the implementation by Electric Boat (the contractor for the Seawolf Class) of computer-aided design and manufacturing (CAD/CAM).

When the Cold War ended and talk of downsizing the military began, folks in the submarine business wondered what would happen if the United States stopped building submarines. Some reasoned that we really didn't need any more submarines for another 20 years.

Nuclear reactors were lasting longer and performing better than expected. In 1992, the George Bush administration reduced the Seawolf program to the single submarine (SSN-21) then under construction, shutting down the planned production of 29 ships in the class.

But, here's the problem. Submarines have an incredibly long design/build cycle. It takes years to build a submarine using even the most advanced technology and submarines have a finite lifetime to ensure safe, reliable operation—about 30 years. To allow the submarine industrial base (shipyards, designers, workers, shore-based facilities) to erode and disappear would be to doom any new submarine program that might be required at some point in the future. It just takes too long to gear-up for this level of expertise. Furthermore, studies clearly indicated that three Seawolf Class submarines and the NSSN would be required to sustain a submarine force adequate in size to meet the nation's projected needs. In the interest of national security, how could legislators allow this important segment of the shipbuilding industry to disappear? In the end, they couldn't. After much debate within Congress and strong support by the Navy, legislators approved funding for two additional submarines in the Seawolf class.

Work on the Seawolf will serve as a bridge to the next generation of U.S. Navy attack submarines. The Navy announced in 1991 plans for a new class of submarine, then code-named Centurion. This program is known today as the New Attack Submarine, or NSSN.

## The NSSN

The driving forces behind the design and construction of the New Attack Submarine (NSSN) are flexibility and affordability. One of the biggest contributors to cost is an intangible known as "time." Efficiencies have been found in the areas of planning, design, and revisions. To do this, engineers are relying on new design tools like those used by the Boeing Company to build its 777 airliner.

Like Boeing's airliner, the first NSSN will be digitally designed using computer aided design/manufacture

Scheduled for a 1998 construction start, the NSSN is being optimized for maximum technological and operational flexibility. When the lead ship of the class joins the Navy's fleet in 2004, it will reflect the commitment to engineer the proper balance between advanced technologies and affordability. *General Dynamics Electric Boat Division*

and three-dimensional modeling. The design team will be able to use virtual reality to review and evaluate its product long before any components are ever assembled. This reduces costs and development time, and permits users (submariners) to "look" at what's been designed. In some cases, users have already spotted problems in these initial stages. Officials expect to save hundreds of millions of dollars and cut up to four years off the design/build time by using computer-aided design techniques from the aircraft and automotive industries.

In order to ensure preservation of the submarine industrial base and to encourage competition toward even more advanced design, the plan calls for two shipyards to share in the design and production of the first four NSSNs. Electric Boat (a division of General Dynamics), with facilities at Groton, Connecticut, and Quonset Point, Rhode Island, will build the first (fiscal year 1998) and third (fiscal year 2000) NSSNs; and Newport News Shipbuilding and Drydock Company, in Newport News, Virginia, will build the second (fiscal year 1999) and fourth (fiscal year 2001) NSSNs.

The first NSSN shall be more advanced than the last of the Seawolf Class (SSN-23), and each subsequent NSSN design shall be more capable and affordable than its predecessor. The heat is really on to keep the submarine building business high-tech, efficient, and affordable to the taxpayer.

The NSSN will move submariners rapidly into the 21st century. The first NSSN—expected delivery in 2002—will have the following improvements: open systems architecture (networks, operating systems, graphics, and protocols widely available in the public domain); fiber-optic cable systems that can be easily plugged-in and unplugged; commercial off-the-shelf (COTS) electronics (to take advantage of the rapidly advancing improvements in signal and information processing and display technologies); a reconfigurable torpedo room; large logistic hatches; vibration reducer; lightweight, wide-aperture array (hull-mounted sonar made up of three flat panels on each side of the submarine); automated self-protection; non-penetrating periscopes; a marine laser gyro with no moving parts; high-speed emergency diesel; advanced battery.

The NSSN will carry the TB-29 towed array system, the most advanced system available. The towed array (a sonar tool) is a group of sensitive hydrophones attached to the end of a long cable pulled behind the submarine. It can detect what are called "quiet contacts."

The NSSN will be able to support covert special warfare missions (search-and-rescue, intelligence and reconnaissance, sabotage and diversionary tactics). The NSSN will have a specially designed chamber to lodge SEAL teams and their equipment. The NSSN can be configured to support a dry deck shelter. This portable structure attaches to the exterior of the submarine and is used to deploy the advanced swimmer delivery system (ASDS), a mini-submarine that can carry eight SEALs, their equipment, and a two-man crew.

The NSSN's modular sail construction is revolutionary, allowing easy maintenance and reconfiguration of the masts to fit the mission. Masts include surface search radar; electronic support measures; radio antennae; snorkel mast; and phototonics periscopes using state-of-the-art video cameras.

The NSSN will have 12 vertical launch tubes from which to fire Tomahawk missiles. The Tomahawk is a sub-sonic, long-range cruise missile used against surface ships or land targets. The Navy is investigating the feasibility of launching the Army's ATCAMS (tactical ballistic missiles) from these vertical launch tubes. The Harpoon, an anti-ship cruise missile, has been encapsulated to support launch from the submarine's torpedo tubes.

The mission of the NSSN includes clandestine strike; intelligence gathering and surveillance; anti-submarine warfare; anti-surface ship warfare; carrier battle group support; special forces operations; clandestine mining; and mine reconnaissance. These are all traditional missions of the submarine force. According to Rear Adm. Dennis A. Jones, director of submarine warfare in the office of the Chief of Naval Operations, "the NSSN is the first U.S. submarine designed specifically to satisfy the broad spectrum of regional and near-land mission needs identified by the Department of Defense for the post-Cold War era." Furthermore, the NSSN's modular design will permit timely incorporation of the latest, best, and most affordable technology.

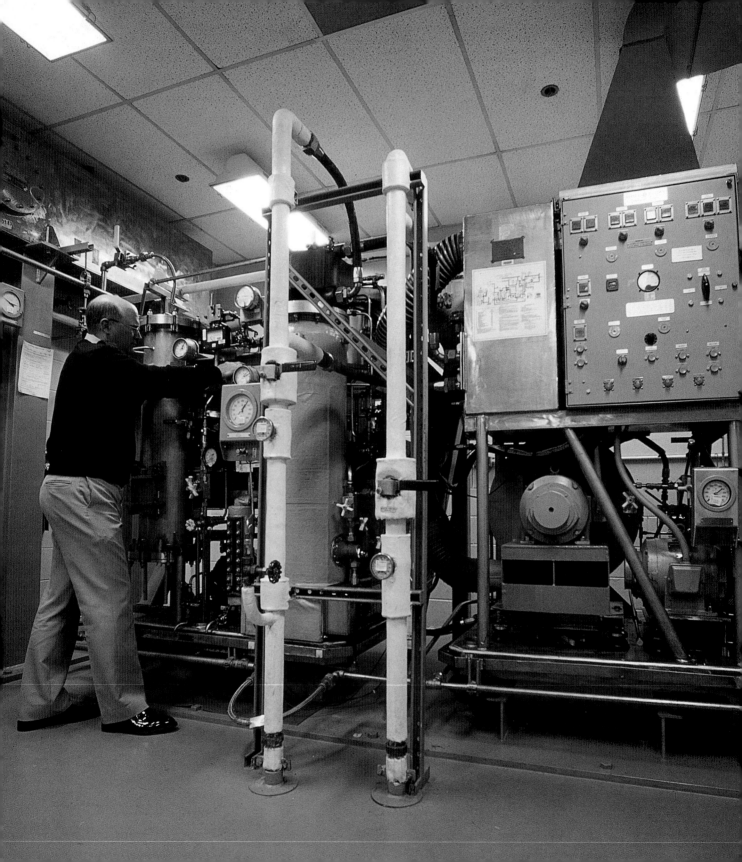

## —● FOUR ●—

# TRAINING

Over 70 years ago, Navy recruiters were given the following guidelines for selecting new submarine recruits: ". . . it is necessary that an individual be of at least average intelligence, basically indoctrinated in mathematics and physics and anxious to do well in the work. Secondly, the individual must have an extremely high degree of motivation for submarines. He must be an emotionally mature individual who can exercise good judgment, keep his head in emergencies, be reliable and trustworthy in the performance of his duties and accept the close confinement and cramped living conditions of submarine life."

*"Everything we do is by procedure. We don't mess around— we don't wing it."*
*Instructor, Naval Submarine School*

All sailors (men only) who go into submarines do so as volunteers. They volunteer to join the Navy; then they volunteer to join the sub force. Sailors are screened in boot camp for suitability. They're given psychological exams, they must meet high academic standards, and they must show an ability to handle a high-tech environment. Because of the relatively small size of the submarine fleet and crews (only about 3 percent of the Navy), only those sailors scoring in the top 1 percent of their entry testing are eligible for selection as future members of the submarine Navy.

Aspiring submariners begin their training at Naval Submarine School, Submarine Base New

The EOG (Electrolytic Oxygen Generator) Lab is where trainees learn about the pieces of equipment that enable the crew to remain submerged indefinitely. Scrubbers and burners remove and destroy the impurities and toxins from the submarine's atmosphere, including exhaled carbon dioxide, cigarette smoke, and cooking fumes, to name but a few. Breathable air is created from seawater. First, salts and minerals are removed to create potable water, distilled water, and pure water. The pure water is further broken down into its molecular components of hydrogen (vented overboard) and oxygen (recirculated as breathable air). The only other vehicle that manufactures its own air is the Space Shuttle.

At Naval Submarine Base, San Diego, an instructor in the Fire Trainer demonstrates the correct method to extinguish an electrical fire onboard a submarine. The Fire Trainer replicates a hull section of a submarine. Propane gas jets are installed throughout the simulator and can be programmed according to the requirements of the exercise. Smoke and darkness also add to the reality of the training.

London, in Groton, Connecticut. This institution has a tradition reaching back to 1916. The training facility handles 40,000 students annually, conducting up to 300 different courses ranging in length from one day to six months. Students include enlisted men with no experience in submarines, submarine commanders taking advanced courses, and everyone in between. Students are taught all there is to know about submarine tactics, navigation, administration, communications, weapons, and maintenance. Classes can last from the five weeks of Basic Enlisted Submarine School through the 67 weeks of Cryptography Apprentice Training.

In addition to classroom settings, the training facility boasts state-of-the-art simulators and trainers, costing millions of dollars to design and develop, to provide realistic individual and team training. The Naval Submarine School is accredited by the New England Association of Schools and Colleges.

Basic Enlisted Submarine School (BESS) lasts about five weeks and teaches the basics of working aboard a submarine. Here, the environment may be

The Fire Trainer is a mock-up of an interior hull section of a submarine. This exercise simulates a hull insulation fire, extinguished correctly with water.

A dive trainer for submariners is comparable to a flight simulator for aviators. This entire trainer is mounted on pivots that will simulate any attitude a sub might assume. The instructor, wearing whites, is trying to maintain his footing, while his students are simulating an emergency blow. Here in the trainer, as well as onboard every submarine, the forward seats are equipped with seat belts like those used on a commercial airliner. The visible ceiling and horizontal moldings on the rear wall of the classroom indicate more dramatically the angle of this simulator as it "surfaces."

less strict than what students experienced in basic training, but the academic requirements are much more demanding. All students must study a minimum of 2 hours each night. Those who score less than 80 percent on weekly exams are grilled by a panel of senior enlisted and officer staff members, concerned about mediocre performance. Immediate improvement is expected.

Beyond BESS, individuals progress through training courses within a technical specialty: Electrician's Mate (EM); Electronics Technician (ET); Fire Control Technician (FT); Interior Communications (IC); Machinist's Mate (MM); Missile Technician (MT); Quartermaster (QM); Radioman (RM); Torpedoman's Mate (TM); or Sonar Technician (ST).

Experienced sailors return to the training facility on a regular basis to upgrade their skills and to remain proficient in skills acquired earlier in their careers. Both Atlantic and Pacific Fleets have shore-based training facilities—crew members are always involved in some kind of training. It's part of the process to keep readiness at the highest level. And now, more than ever, the need to stay abreast of changing computer technology is essential.

In the Ship Control Trainer, or "dive trainer," the trainees are confronted with instrument readings they might encounter while underway. The large, square section in front of each sailor is actually a computer screen. The trainer is programmed to simulate possible situations aboard various classes of submarines. The gauges appropriate to each submarine design are displayed on the monitor.

## Simulators & Trainers

Training on the best ways to handle casualties is also taught at the training facilities utilizing simulators. Such casualty training includes fire, leaks, flooding, loss of electrical power, loss of nuclear power, a broken pump, or a computer program that won't run.

## Putting Out Fires

A fire on board a submarine is an extremely serious casualty. Because of the modern equipment (computers) and weaponry (missiles and torpedoes!) onboard, it's important that the crew be trained in all aspects of firefighting. The best place to practice firefighting is in the fire trainer. Instruction begins in the

Blasting caps are carefully installed in the fiberglass dome that covers the end of a Trident missile. When the missile is launched, these caps are detonated, fracturing the dome. Escaping nitrogen—used to pressurize the missile tube—pushes the pieces of broken dome aside as the missile rises to the surface.

The topside lab in the Trident Training Facility has a full-length Trident missile tube and deck hatch. Here an instructor, wearing whites, watches a team of Missile Technicians as they service the "blue bubble"—the fiberglass dome that covers the missile.

# HOW DOES A SUBMARINE DIVE AND SURFACE?

Buoyancy is the tendency of a body to float, rise, or sink when submerged in a fluid. There are three states of buoyancy: negative, positive, and neutral. A submarine can travel or hover at any depth. Here is an extremely simplified explanation of how this works.

A series of Main Ballast Tanks, fore and aft, enable the submarine to take on water to make it heavy, or to pump out water to make it light. (Ballast tanks on a Los Angeles Class submarine hold up to 421,000 pounds of seawater, or 49,000 gallons, approximately.)

The submarine has negative buoyancy when the Main Ballast Tanks are flooded with seawater entering from vents on her underside. As the water floods into the tanks, air is forced out through upper vents. With this shift, the submarine becomes heavier than the seawater surrounding it, and sinks deeper. A system of trim tanks allows the "fine tuning" of this balance.

When high-pressure air is blown into the ballast tanks, the water is pushed out through the lower floodports. With this shift, the submarine becomes lighter than the seawater surrounding it, and rises. This is called positive buoyancy.

When a perfect balance is achieved, the weight of the submarine equals the weight of the seawater surrounding it. This is called neutral buoyancy. The submarine neither sinks, nor rises, but hovers at a specific depth. Crew members must still work to keep the submarine "in trim."

Dive planes and rudders are used to guide a moving submarine through the water. The submarine dives with its front dive planes pointing downward, and its rear dive planes pointing up. The submarine rises with its front dive planes pointing up, and its rear dive planes pointing down. Stern rudders steer the sub right and left.

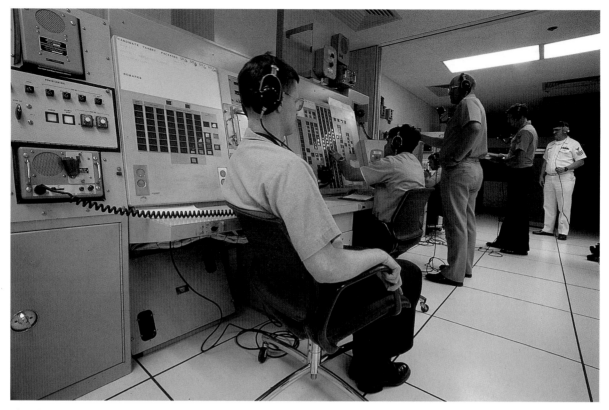

This classroom at the Trident Training Facility replicates the Missile Control Center onboard an Ohio Class submarine. The MCC Lab is comprised of two major functions—fire control (programming and transmitting information to the electronic components within the missile itself) and launcher control (ensuring that the physical conditions within each missile are at optimum and that all hydraulic functions are working properly).

classroom, where students are introduced to the types of fires they could encounter, instructed in the proper methods for extinguishing those fires, and shown how to use the many pieces of equipment and protective gear used to fight a fire.

Once the classroom instruction is completed, it's time for students to put on their FFEs (Firefighting Ensembles) and play fireman. This has the potential to be a very hazardous exercise. That's why it takes at least six men to conduct the drill: three instructors, one staging supervisor, one monitor, and one safety chief. These six experienced instructors watch over a fire team of 12 students who must work together to put out the fire.

The closed environment of the fire trainer replicates a hull section on a submarine. The trainer can simulate three possible fire casualties: an electrical fire, a bilge fire (oil), and a hull insulation fire. The training instructor at the Operator Terminal in another room can control

The Missile Compartment Sub System Lab at the Trident Training Facility teaches 4-man teams of MTs how to monitor their equipment under casualty conditions throughout a launch sequence. The team leader is on the phones in communication with other stations. Other team members monitor hydraulic and gas functions. This realistic trainer gives submariners a good idea of what it's like to launch a weapon.

The Damage Control Wet Team Trainer, or "Get Wet" Trainer, simulates a flooded compartment with leaking high pressure pipes. Crew members must work as a team to locate and patch the leaks. A safety monitor is in the flooded compartment with them. A video camera is mounted above, seen here in the upper left of the frame. Other instructors monitor the exercise through one-way glass in an adjacent control center.

numerous variables. He can set the fire, introduce smoke, and set a timer to extinguish the fire. He can conduct the exercise with or without lights, with or without smoke, and with or without ventilation. He can monitor the temperature, propane levels (propane gas is used for these simulated fire drills), and communication. The students must secure power and select the correct agent to fight the fire. Safety monitors observe the students using infrared thermal imagers which enable them to see through smoke and in darkness.

Onboard the submarine, the scenario should go like this. A man on duty discovers a fire. He announces this fact by sounding an alarm, puts on an emergency air breathing (EAB) apparatus placed strategically throughout the sub, and begins to fight the fire. His fire team buddies, or others nearby, arrive. The fire should be out within 30 to 60 seconds. On the submarine, everyone is trained and everyone responds.

### Controlling Leaks & Flooding

Another essential exercise for students in Basic Enlisted Submarine School is the wet trainer located in the damage control facility. Here, students learn how to control leaks and flooding. Unwanted excess water within a submarine in any place but the ballast tanks presents a real threat. Excess water makes the submarine heavy and she begins to sink deeper into the ocean, either running aground or descending past her crush depth.

In the classroom, students are lectured and then given an opportunity to practice various methods of patching leaks of different sizes on sample sections of pipe. Finally, the students get to implement what they've learned under very wet, real-life conditions.

The training space for the final phase of this training exercise simulates a submarine engine room as it begins to flood due to various prearranged leaks. On one side of this large, enclosed area is a big glass window. Instructors observe the students through the window as they attempt to identify, locate, and control the leaks. Springing from pipe leaks located throughout the area, up to 20,000 gallons of water flowing at a rate of

1,200 gallons per minute, can be pumped into the compartment. Students practice damage control as well as teamwork and communication. Prospective officers also receive this training. Everyone gets wet.

## Escape

In 1991, a new escape training facility was dedicated at the Naval Submarine School, New London. Within the building known as Momsen Hall—named for the late Vice Adm. Charles B. Momsen, a pioneer in sub escape technology—are two escape trunks like those found on a Sturgeon class submarine. The purpose of this training is to let submariners experience a free ascent from a submerged and disabled submarine.

In the training facility, two escape hatches are located below a specially constructed indoor swimming pool. Students enter the escape hatch from below, just like they would on a real submarine. Each wears a Steinke hood—a combination life jacket and breathing apparatus that fits over the head. They close the hatch below them to seal off the submarine from the interior of the escape hatch that will soon be flooded with water. With their Steinke hoods in place, they open the upper hatch, and struggle out and up to the surface of the pool.

Such an ascent can be made from depths up to about 400 feet. For deeper depths, it is necessary to escape via a DSRV (Deep Submergence Rescue Vehicle). The escape trunk is also used to release divers into the water at shallower depths for routine exterior hull inspections while at sea or for special operations.

Students take their studies seriously. They don't want to jeopardize in any way the safety of their shipmates. Instructors uphold high standards in the classroom, knowing that they may find themselves assigned again to a submarine with some of their students on board.

## Ship Control Trainer

This trainer simulates the forward port section of the Control Center onboard a submarine. Students learn about the drive functions of the submarine: bal-

# DOLPHINS

The origin of the dolphin insignia dates back to 1912, when Captain Ernest J. King suggested that a distinguishing device for qualified submariners be adopted. He submitted his own pen and ink sketch for consideration. The design elements of this sketch were combined with those submitted by a Philadelphia firm that had been contracted to create a suitable badge. The final design was approved in 1924 by Theodore Roosevelt, Jr., then acting Secretary of the Navy.

The device depicts the bow view of a submarine cruising on the surface, with bow planes rigged for diving, flanked by dolphins in a horizontal position with their heads resting on the upper edges of the bow planes. Officers wear a gold-plated bronze pin and enlisted men wear a silver-plated bronze pin.

Earning one's Dolphins is the first goal of any would-be submariner. They signify that the wearer is qualified in submarines, that he understands every system on board and can be relied upon in any emergency. It's quite an accomplishment, but represents only the first step in every submariner's ongoing training and education.

last, diving, surfacing, turning. The ship control trainers are on hydraulic lifts to simulate the feeling of diving, surfacing, and turning underwater.

The ship control operation trainer (SCOT) for the new Seawolf Class is like nothing any veteran submariner has ever seen. It is the most complex simulator ever set up by the Navy. It incorporates the latest off-the-shelf computer software and hardware available. The Seawolf trainer uses flat panel displays. The student can call up various situations and then have quick, easy access to specific data relating to that scenario. In addition, this trainer replicates more realistically what the submarine is doing. The young sailors who come here for training are very comfortable with the environment—it reminds them of the video arcade. These trainers were in use even before the first Seawolf ever hit the water.

## High-Tech Trainers

AN/BSY-1 (pronounced "busy-one") is one of the more recent computerized functions introduced into the submarine. The BSY-1 trainer is a $70 million tactical combat control simulator. It combines target detection, classification, tracking, weapons control, and weapons launch in one system. BSY-1 went into the Flight III 688s (Improved Los Angeles Class), and has already been upgraded (BSY-2) for the Seawolf Class.

At Sub School New London, students receive computer-based classroom training at a series of workstations. These monitors realistically depict various

A submarine commanding officer at attention during a change of command ceremony. His gold Dolphins are pinned above his left pocket. Below his medals is a Fleet Ballistic Missile Breast Pin Award. It depicts a silver LaFayette Class submarine with superimposed Polaris missile and electron rings. A scroll beneath the submarine is designed to hold stars—one star for each successful patrol, and one bronze star for five successful patrols. The gold star beneath this device indicates that the individual is presently in command of a submarine.

situations sailors can expect to see on board in the Control Center. Instead of flipping a switch or turning a dial, the student uses interactive touch-screen methods to progress through the training module. They go at their own pace, pausing to review if necessary.

The workstations also provide realistic sonar training. In the trainer, students listen to the sounds of dolphins, shrimp, whales (called "biologics"), and propellers of various surface ships and submarines. The computer-based training at Naval Submarine School gives students a head start into this very interesting and important specialty. The trainer accelerates the sonar technician's learning curve, introducing him to more "sounds" during training than he might otherwise encounter during a routine patrol. The ability to decipher these noises from the deep is an art as well as a science.

## The Electronic Classroom

One of the most impressive classrooms is the BSY-2 Electronic Classroom. It supports the technology aboard the Navy's newest submarine, Seawolf (SSN-21). The BSY-2 classroom is paperless—no notebooks, no printed technical manuals, no paper instruction guides—because the Seawolf is designed to be a paperless ship. Instead, everyone is connected electronically.

Each student has a CD-ROM player at his workstation and all ten student workstations are connected to the instructor's platform. Off-the-shelf Windows software enables a student to work through the entire manual at his workstation. With the click of the mouse, all technical data and reference material pops up on his screen—no more chasing down the correct publication and leafing through it to locate a section.

Students "take notes" by entering the information onto their computer screens. The notes are saved in the appropriate lesson plan for future reference. Even test taking is all electronic. The instructor transmits each test directly to the student's workstation. The student takes the test and sends it back electronically to the instructor. The instructor grades the test, makes comments, and indicates instructional material the student should review. These final results are sent back to the student's workstation.

## The Human Factor

When a student completes Sub School, he's assigned to a submarine. Here, he's low man on the totem pole. His greatest fear is of being "the new guy." Will he be accepted? Can he prove himself? Now begins his qualification period. It takes about one year to qualify in submarines, to learn all the ship's systems—to earn the Dolphins. Earning one's Dolphins is the first big goal for all new submariners. Petty Officers and officers oversee the progress of each new arrival.

But it's not over. Earning one's Dolphins is only the first achievement in an ongoing series of qualifications to make each man more and more proficient at what he does, thus more valuable to the rest of the crew and to the mission. Submariners never stop learning or honing their skills.

## Training Paths: Officers and Enlisted Men

Submarine officers are all university graduates with degrees in engineering or in the hard sciences. Most officers are graduates of the U.S. Naval Academy or one of many universities throughout the United States as participants in campus ROTC programs. A final point of entry into submarines as an officer is by volunteering for OCS (Officers Candidate School).

Prospective submarine officers are selected by the Director, Naval Reactors (DNR). First to hold this position—and to encounter the men who had the nerve to suppose they might be qualified to someday command a nuclear submarine—was Hyman G. Rickover himself. It's unlikely that today's candidates suffer quite the degree of psychological torment imposed by the feared and revered father of the nuclear Navy, but the interviews remain demanding and thorough.

Once past this hurdle, candidates make their first trip to Naval Submarine Base New London, Groton, Connecticut. Here, officers attend SOBC (Submarine Officers Basic Course) which lasts about 3 months. This is their introduction to the many systems on board the submarine. They go through all the trainers, just like their enlisted counterparts.

Officers and enlisted men who are accepted to work with nuclear propulsion systems first go through a specialized training program at the Nuclear Propulsion Training Command in Orlando, Florida. Enlisted men complete a 2-month boot camp

The silver Dolphins of a high ranking enlisted man are worn above the following medals: Meritorious Service Medal; Navy Commendation Medal (3); Navy Achievement Medal (2); Navy Unit Commendation; Meritorious Unit Commendation; Navy "E" Ribbon; Good Conduct Medal (5); Navy Expeditionary Medal; National Defense Service Medal; Vietnam Service Medal; Sea Service Deployment Ribbon; Republic of Vietnam Civil Actions Unit Citation. He also wears the Fleet Ballistic Missile Breast Pin Award. The device below shows that he is Command Master Chief at a Naval Submarine Base.

and a 4-6 month Nuclear Field "A" School. Enlisted men and officers attend Nuclear Power School, an intensive 6-month classroom phase. Enlisted men and officers attend Nuclear Prototype Training, a 6-month course in the hands-on operation of a nuclear power plant in a prototype.

The prototype, located in Ballston Spa, New York, replicates the reactor plant in the engineering spaces of a submarine or surface ship. The prototype is housed in a big building at ground level. A 6-month "in-hull phase" follows. This training environment more closely resembles that of a submarine, since the power plant here is actually housed in the engineering spaces of a decommissioned submarine floating in the water.

When the nuclear training is complete, an enlisted man will go to the fleet or on to another school. An enlisted man who goes through this intensive training will already be a valuable member of any crew, and does not have to go through BESS before being assigned to a submarine. At various stages throughout his career, he will have a chance to go through other trainers like the wet trainer and the fire trainer. Men who have gone through the Nuclear School pipeline will be forever known as "nucs" (pronounced "nukes").

In the case of an officer, he'll go through Submarine School to gain a complete understanding of what the other guys are doing in "the front of the boat."

Once an officer has completed his basic training, he is assigned to a submarine for a period of about 2-3 years. Here, he will serve as a junior officer, experiencing and observing what goes on aboard a submarine and qualifying as a watchstander on numerous watch stations. His main goal is to qualify for his Dolphins—the insignia that says he is submarine qualified. This means more studying and passing exams on all equipment, systems, and procedures on the submarine. It's also during this time that senior officers will begin to observe and evaluate his potential as a commanding officer.

The next major hurdle for an aspiring submarine commander is passing the Engineer's Exam. His next assignment would be as Chief Engineer aboard a submarine. Upon his return from sea duty, the officer will be sent to shore duty at one of many possible assignments—postgraduate school, staff duty, or as an instructor in one of the training facilities throughout the country.

After completion of this shore duty assignment, the officer will return to the Naval Submarine School in Groton, Connecticut, to attend SOAC (Submarine Officers Advanced Course). This 6-month course will prepare him for a department head level position aboard a submarine in engineering, navigation, operations, or weapons. He will then be assigned to a submarine as a department head for about 3 years.

The officer will be screened for the position of Executive Officer (XO) before attending the 3-month PXO (Prospective Executive Officer) Course which will qualify him for this position aboard a fast attack submarine (SSN) or ballistic missile submarine (SSBN).

Having served as an Executive Officer aboard a submarine, he will return to a shore duty assignment, during which time he will be screened for Commanding Officer before attending the PCO (Prospective Commanding Officers) Course. The curriculum includes tactical and operational courses on commanding a U.S. nuclear submarine. Courses are 6-months in length and ensure an officer's proficiency with weapons (torpedoes, missiles, mines) and with missions (anti-submarine warfare, anti-shipping, mining, strike warfare, intelligence gathering). The PCO course qualifies an officer to command a submarine.

By the time an officer is assigned to command his own submarine, he has had years of experience at sea, in shore duty assignments, and in the classroom. The young men who serve at sea under his leadership should feel confident that he's the man to lead them into battle or on a safe and successful peacetime mission. The Captain of the submarine, with his "unmatched burden of isolation," is the individual to whom all look for guidance. The Captain sets the tone and everything flows from his example and leadership style—he's The Man.

# ⬤ FIVE

# LIVING ON SUBMARINES

The challenge is to find time to get everything done. The first step is to cut 6 hours out of the day. Once underway, the crew of a submarine operates according to an 18-hour clock. A sailor stands a 6-hour watch, works another 6-hour shift doing other things around the boat (maintenance, cleaning, studying), and then sleeps for 6 hours. Of course, it doesn't always work out that smoothly. In fact, many submariners often find themselves in a prolonged state of sleep deprivation. The schedule can be tightened even more by going to a "port & starboard" watch—6 hours on watch; 6 hours off.

There's a natural tendency to want to know whether it's day or night. After a while, this knowledge becomes completely irrelevant. The only clue may be what's being served in the mess. Submariners are in

*"Underway . . . the only way."*
*Anonymous Hard Core Submariner*

their own universe, cut off from what all other landlocked folks are doing back home on terra firma. There are no portholes, no salt air in your face, no sounds of seagulls flying overhead. You're in a big government office building that, when submerged, doesn't feel like it's even moving. The blowers are always blowing and the lights are on everywhere except in the berthing areas, where it's dark, quiet, and cool.

Some people think submariners must be just a little crazy to do what they do—submariners themselves often agree. How else can you explain someone's willingness to board a seagoing vessel that will be "sunk" intentionally and told to roam the ocean's depths for weeks and months at a time? Some people think there's something creepy about disappearing into the dark and hostile big blue of the ocean.

The Officer of the Deck oversees the maneuvering watch. In the Control Center below him, crew members at their assigned watch stations perform specific duties to ensure a safe trip to the dive point.

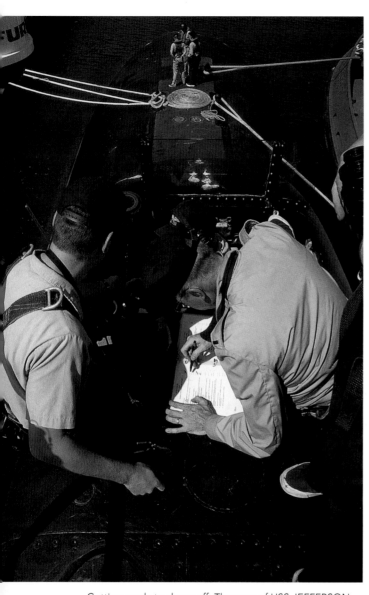

Getting ready to shove off. The crew of USS JEFFERSON CITY (SSN-759) completes a final checklist in the same way an aircrew runs through a pre-flight on an aircraft. One of two tugboats is visible in position on the right; line handlers are on deck wearing life vests. Let the fun begin.

RIGHT: The maneuvering watch. Transiting the surface is one of the most hazardous evolutions for any submarine. Here, a sailor checks the horizon for surface traffic in the area. He's tethered to a temporary railing with a body harness. He's wearing rubber-soled canvas deck shoes. Extended up behind him like two tall trees are masts sheathed in protective metal casings painted in camouflage (medium gray with dark gray mottle) to break up their outline while at sea. The bulges on the sail at his feet are other retracted masts and antennae.

These same people, however, consider it perfectly sane for astronauts to orbit the earth, for scientists to repair telescopes in outer space, and for ordinary folks to take the red-eye from L.A. to Chicago at just under Mach 1.

There is, however, a certain mystique surrounding submariners. Images of Jules Verne, stories about U-Boats, and Hollywood's perspective–from John Wayne to Denzel Washington–all influence how we think about the men who make up the crews of America's submarine force. Although some vestiges of the old seafaring days remain, today's crews are dedicated and reliable high-tech professionals. It must have something to do with the mental stimulation of making so many pieces of machinery and computer gear all work together–a sort of geek and "Tool Time" heaven.

## Drills

All daily activities are directed toward keeping the submarine running efficiently and safely–ready at a moment's notice to launch weapons. This simple goal makes for a relentless schedule of training and drills. Drills enable crew members to practice proper responses to specific situations; measure and improve their skills; and reinforce teamwork and communication. The idea is to make certain behaviors automatic. When the real thing happens, they know just what to do and do it automatically. In a hostile environment, there's no time to open the book. All drills are done in a controlled environment and all drills must be

There has just been a minor injury to one of the dock workers during a food load on USS ASHEVILLE (SSN-758), which explains why everyone seems to have stopped working. The food stores and supplies on the dock will be painstakingly loaded by hand onto the ASHEVILLE through a single logistics hatch.

approved by the Commanding Officer. Specific guidelines are established for how the drill is to be carried out, how the crew is supposed to respond, and at what point a drill safety monitor should intervene.

The Chief Petty Officers use their ingenuity to simulate casualties (things that go wrong on the boat) while underway. Over the years these seasoned sub-

mariners have devised creative ways to indicate the nature of any emergency. Flashing strobe lights may mean fire; hairnets over the EAB (Emergency Air Breathing) masks obstruct vision and simulate smoke; air pumped through a hose simulates the sound of rushing water. Large quantities of colored poly strips are sometimes used to simulate flooding. Blue poly indicates a fresh water flood; green poly indicates sea water. Instrument readings can be changed by placing covers over them displaying a reading that would create an emergency for the operator. Drill monitors observe the crew members to see how well they respond to each situation.

Drills, studying, and practice help prepare the crew for periodic inspections which can last for days at a time. The Tactical Weapons Proficiency (TWP) exam is a two day evolution during which time the Fire Control party tracks moving targets in the firing range and launches practice weapons. The crew is evaluated on how well they perform. A good evaluation is an enormous source of pride and a huge boost to morale. It's also a necessity for the career aspirations of the officers on board.

Other major exams and inspections include the Engineering Examination, an Operations & Navigation Examination, the Tactical Readiness Evaluation (TRE), and the Operational Reactor Safeguards Examination (ORSE). Smart crews work all the time preparing for these evaluations, even if they're months away. This ensures a higher level of readiness in all departments, with all systems.

## Safety

A submarine is an industrial site. Gigantic pieces of machinery are housed within the submarine. They ensure the survivable environment for the crew and maintain and launch weapons. Hazards are everywhere. The exposed internal structure of a submarine—cables, wiring, tubes, ducts, pumps, generators, gauges, pipes, valves, blowers—reminds each sailor that this is an inherently dangerous place to be.

Safety is on everyone's mind. Anything that can go wrong at an industrial facility on shore can go wrong on a submarine. Visual reminders—warnings, fire extinguishers, emergency procedures and equipment—are found throughout the sub. All systems are monitored 24 hours a day. Everyone is responsible for something—and everything. Submariners tend to be

Large cans of food are duct taped together in groups of three (four cans would be too big to fit through) and then lowered below through the open hatch.

There's only one way in and one way out. Here, weights for the trash canisters are being lowered into the submarine. Weighted canisters of compacted trash are ejected into the ocean while underway. Since trash disposal makes noise, the timing of this chore is critical. The weights ensure that the trash canisters sink to the bottom of the ocean.

better cross-trained than their surface Navy counterparts, because in this environment, no casualty may be left unattended for long.

### Esprit de Corps

Submarine crews have a relaxed, but professional approach to what they do. Officers and enlisted men work shoulder to shoulder, around the clock. In such close quarters, some aspects of protocol are set aside. On a big surface ship, a young sailor may know who the commanding officer is, but may rarely see him, let alone have a conversation with him. On a submarine, this same sailor will

RIGHT: USS PORTSMOUTH (SSN-707) is being escorted by tugboat out of San Diego bay. Crew members are dressed in "poopie suits" and green life vests and all eyes are directed toward the Chief of the Boat, Rick West, giving instructions. A diver is stationed on the aft deck for all departures. The bulge along the starboard side of the hull is the shroud for the towed sonar array. While at sea, people working on deck hook their safety harnesses into the visible track along the length of the shroud.

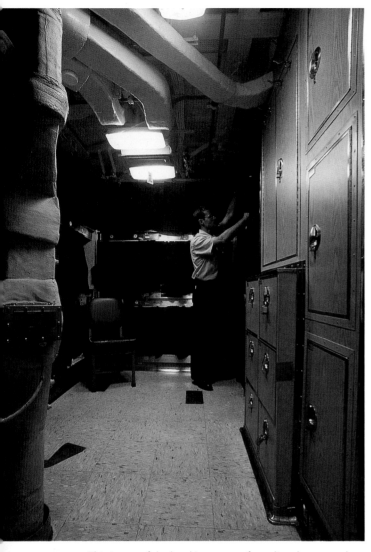

This is one of the berthing spaces for enlisted personnel aboard an Ohio Class submarine. Each space has nine bunks, or racks, each with a heavy, dark curtain that can be drawn for privacy. Each bunk space is furnished with an air vent, an electrical outlet, and a reading light. Enlisted crew berthing is located in the missile compartment on the third level—thought to be the quietest location on the submarine. The dark rectangular and triangular patches on the floor indicate emergency oxygen plugs directly above. The patches are made of a rough material that can be located in the dark by foot.

bump into the CO on a daily basis, and may speak to him often at length.

Good natured teasing abounds and almost everyone gets a nickname eventually. Submariners tease each other mercilessly. It's a stress reliever. It's very helpful to have a good sense of humor. Being a loner is not a successful coping strategy.

Interaction between members of the crew often resembles that of a family. The men develop bonds with their shipmates that one rarely finds in the workplace of "nine-to-fivers." Despite some of the drawbacks to serving aboard a submarine, crew members nearly always mention the close relationships they have with their fellow shipmates. They mention how much they enjoy the camaraderie of the environment; the notion of teamwork. Every day has the potential to be Super Bowl Sunday when you're underway deep beneath the ocean's surface. This is one place where winning is, indeed, everything.

### The Chief of the Boat

One of the most influential men besides the commanding officer aboard any submarine is the Chief of the Boat. He's the Senior Chief Petty Officer on the crew. He often has more years of submarine experience than the Commanding Officer. He's a person who has not only achieved levels of excellence in the operation of a submarine, but who, because of his personality and people skills, is highly respected both by enlisted men and officers. He's the liaison between the captain and the enlisted personnel. It's a big deal to have this job.

Referred to as "the COB" (pronounced "cobb"), the Chief of the Boat is responsible for the morale and welfare of the crew. He's the ultimate problem solver, a coach, and a mentor to his young sailors, especially the new ones. The biggest fear for new sailors is of being the new guy. The COB assures them that everyone on board has done what they'll have to do. They're going to hot bunk, they're going to mess cook, they're going to think they haven't a friend in the world. But the COB and the other Chief Petty Officers will show them the way.

To be accepted, the new guy must come onboard and make his actions speak louder than words. He should qualify for a watch station as soon as possible. He will probably have to give up some of his nights out on the town to do that. The crew is watching because they want to know what the new guy is made of. He has to show some initiative, make good progress toward getting his Dolphins, and stay off the "dink" list. The crew will bring him into the group a lot faster if they can say, "He's a good guy, he's a 'hot runner'—we like him."

All members of the crew can act as coaches for the new guys. The COB makes sure they're coaching the right things and in the correct manner. Gone are the days when the non-qualified newcomer was humiliated and run ragged all over the boat "looking for the water line," or trying to locate a container of "relative bearing grease." Today, there's an emphasis on using one's time wisely, instead of playing lengthy pranks on one another (short pranks are probably still OK).

The Chief of the Boat helps his sailors work through various personal problems they may have while at sea. Generally these are family problems—financial, medical, interpersonal. The home ported squadron does a good job of assisting family members left behind when a submarine leaves on patrol. Unique situations, like a death in the family, are handled appropriately. The Chief of the Boat keeps the Captain informed and makes sure the enlisted men are treated properly and fairly.

## How a Submarine Is Organized

Responsibilities aboard the submarine fit neatly onto an organizational chart, just as they do in any professional corporation. The Commanding Officer is responsible for every aspect of the submarine. With the support of his Executive Officer (second in command) and the Chief of the Boat, the Commanding Officer must successfully carry out whatever missions are assigned.

The Commanding Officer of a Los Angeles Class submarine gets his own stateroom and head. His small stateroom is located just forward of the Control Center and is filled with communications gear.

The Navigation Center aboard USS OHIO (SSBN-726). The D5 Navigation Center features off-the-shelf UNIX workstations, CD ROM software upgrades, and supports the delivery of the Trident II (D5) missile. Boomers based in King's Bay, Georgia, carry the Trident II. Although USS OHIO has been upgraded with the D5 Nav center, she does not carry the Trident II missile.

Reporting to the Commanding Officer are the following departments: Engineering, Navigation, Combat Systems, Operations, Medical, and Supply. Each department is headed by an officer who has successfully completed the various hurdles leading up to and including SOAC, Submarine Officers Advanced Course.

## The Engineering Department

The Engineering Officer, through his junior officers, chiefs, and petty officers, oversees the functions of Propulsion, Electrical, Reactor Control, and Auxiliary. This team runs all the equipment that keeps the submarine moving and her crew working. The engineering spaces occupy the rear half of the submarine and some machinery spaces situated just forward of the reactor compartment.

Within the Engineering Department are Reactor Operators who monitor panels of instruments that indicate the status of the reactor. These spaces in the back end of the boat are restricted and classified. Men in the engine room monitor huge and complex pieces of machinery that push the submarine through the ocean's waters.

The "nucs" also operate the complex systems that make potable, distilled, and pure water from seawater.

Electrician's Mates (EMs) are responsible for all electrical systems throughout the boat. They continuously monitor, troubleshoot, and repair electrical equipment.

The MMs (Machinist's Mates) in Auxiliary—also known as "A-Gangers"—specialize in the operation, maintenance, and repair of mechanical systems. MMs take care of numerous huge pieces of machinery: the emergency diesel generator; the EOG (Electrolytic Oxygen Generator), which makes breathable air for the crew; the burners and scrubbers, which remove impurities and toxins from the circulating air. They also maintain the pumps that move seawater in and out of the ballast tanks. These guys have all the best power and hand tools.

Mess crankin' in the galley is hard work, but a great meal will raise the morale of fellow crew members. In addition to regular meals, plenty of snacks, beverages, and soft-serve ice cream are always available in the mess. There is, of course, no alcohol allowed on board.

## The Navigation Department

Up front in the Control Center, the Navigation Officer ("the Nav") oversees his chiefs and petty officers who plot on maps the course of the submarine. Quartermasters (QMs) continuously monitor the ship's position while at sea, providing navigational data to the Officer of the Deck to support the safe navigation of the submarine. Navigation's equally important mission is to support the delivery of weapons.

## The Combat Systems Department

The Weapons Officer ("Weps") is responsible for the Combat Systems—fire control, weapons (torpedoes, missiles), and sonar. Sonar is a key element in delivering weapons. Using sonar, the submarine recognizes, identifies, and tracks a target. Once the location, direction, and speed of a target are known, the folks in Combat Systems can plot a solution to hit that target. It's a big geometry problem solved by computer programs and manual calculations.

Fire Control Technicians (FTs) specialize in the operation of the ship's tactical weapons control system. They ensure that the tactical weapons systems are ready to fire at a moment's notice.

Missile Technicians (MTs) perform preventive and corrective maintenance on the mechanical and electrical systems supporting various types of missiles. They also specialize in the operation of the ship's strategic weapons control system.

The Torpedoman's Mate or Torpedoman (TM) operates and maintains torpedo tubes and associated tube-launched weapons. TMs ensure proper operation of the torpedo tube system during combat operations, and supervise the movement and reloading of weapons into torpedo tubes.

Sonar Technicians (STs) are the underwater "eyes" of the submarine. Using complex passive and active sonar systems, STs listen to the sounds from the ocean and provide information on the activity outside the submarine.

The wardroom aboard USS OHIO (SSBN-726). The captain and his officers take their meals here, but eat the same food that's being served in the crew's mess. The clock on the wall is nearing 1100 and the table is set for lunch. The receiver and cord of a telephone are visible just below the table edge at the head of the table, where the captain sits. Storage lockers marked EAB contain Emergency Air Breathing devices. The wardroom table can also be used as an operating table—four yellow lights are positioned above the table. The glass carafes contain iced tea, a red liquid known as "bug juice," and pure, delicious water manufactured onboard the submarine. Officers gather in the wardroom for meetings, to complete paperwork, or to watch movies.

## The Operations Department

The Operations Officer heads the department responsible for communications and electronics. In the secure and restricted radio room, encrypted messages are exchanged between the submarine and command centers at home, using numerous sophisticated methods of safely transmitting and receiving messages. All methods of receiving and transmitting messages are designed to thwart an enemy's attempts to intercept them, or to otherwise reveal the submarine's location.

Radiomen (RM) operate, maintain, and troubleshoot the complex communication system aboard the submarine. The ability to receive continuous communications is a critical element of the nuclear deterrence force.

Interior Communications (IC) Electricians specialize in the maintenance and repair of all interior

The crew's mess on a Los Angeles Class submarine is the largest single open space onboard. When meals are not being served, the mess is the gathering place for off-duty submariners. They play cards and board games, read, study, or watch scheduled movies. Meetings are also held here. On Ohio Class submarines, the enlisted crew has its own separate lounge and another separate study area.

communications and sensor circuits onboard the submarine. Their area of expertise includes alarms and control circuits.

Electronics Technicians (ETs) are responsible for all electronic equipment on board the ship. Some personnel are trained to operate and maintain the Nuclear Power Plant, while others specialize in Navigation/Electronic support equipment.

## The Medical Department

The Medical Officer or Corpsman ("the Doc") on board sees the same minor injuries among crew mem-

bers that you might expect to find in any industrial site in America—bumps, bruises, pinched fingers, minor burns, sprains, cuts, aches, pains, and sniffles. His primary concern, though, is the condition of the crew before they go to sea. He reviews the medical records of all crew members to make sure they have had all proper immunizations, have had their dental problems taken care of, and are generally in good health. A serious illness or medical condition can easily jeopardize the submarine's mission if an evacuation is necessary.

In addition, the Doc is the Assistant Radiation Health Officer. Each member of the crew wears a TLD

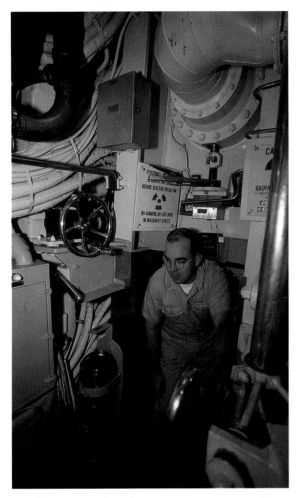

An officer emerges from the engineering spaces on a Los Angeles Class submarine. The "back end of the boat" is classified and off-limits to unauthorized personnel. The engineering spaces occupy the rear half of the submarine, but are rarely seen or discussed with outsiders.

can relieve the guy on duty so he can go for a break, make a head call, or attend a meeting.

## The Supply Department

The division head for Supply is responsible for spare parts and food. The food supply is the only factor limiting the length of time a submarine can remain on patrol. Since attack submarines often surface in foreign ports or U.S. ports abroad, they can replenish their food stores during their deployment. But the Tridents don't surface while on patrol. Instead, they carry enough food to last for around 90 days, but generally return within 75 days.

The Mess Chief on board an SSBN determines what he's going to need on the upcoming patrol. He plans 5 meals per day for 75 days for up to 160 men. For a Trident patrol he will order $125,000-$150,000 worth of dry goods. The cost of frozen foods brings the cost to $250,000. His menus are submitted to a dietitian who evaluates the meals for texture, color, and nutrition (fat, calories, and carbohydrates). The corpsman or medical officer supplies the vitamins for those who want them.

The food for a Trident patrol is packed into 17 Food Modules. Each Food Module measures about 6 x 4 x 5 feet, or 120 cubic feet. These modules are lowered by crane into one of the logistic hatches. (On a Los Angeles Class submarine, everything is lowered by hand down into the submarine through the hatch. Cans are duct-taped together in groups of three and just fit through the hatch opening.)

Food Service Modules are packed with pasta, chili con carne, wax beans, Coca Cola, dried tomatoes, milk shake mix, chow mein vegetables, apple rings, sugar, olive oil, olives, peanut butter, tuna, potatoes, apricots, sugar cones, shortening, coffee, cherry pie

(thermal luminescent dosimeter), a small device containing a simple crystal that measures radiation exposure. He monitors the inserts, mails them off for testing, and provides new ones. It's also helpful if the Medical Officer is qualified to fill in as Chief of the Watch or as Diving Officer of the Watch, even though he may not routinely be assigned to stand watch. He

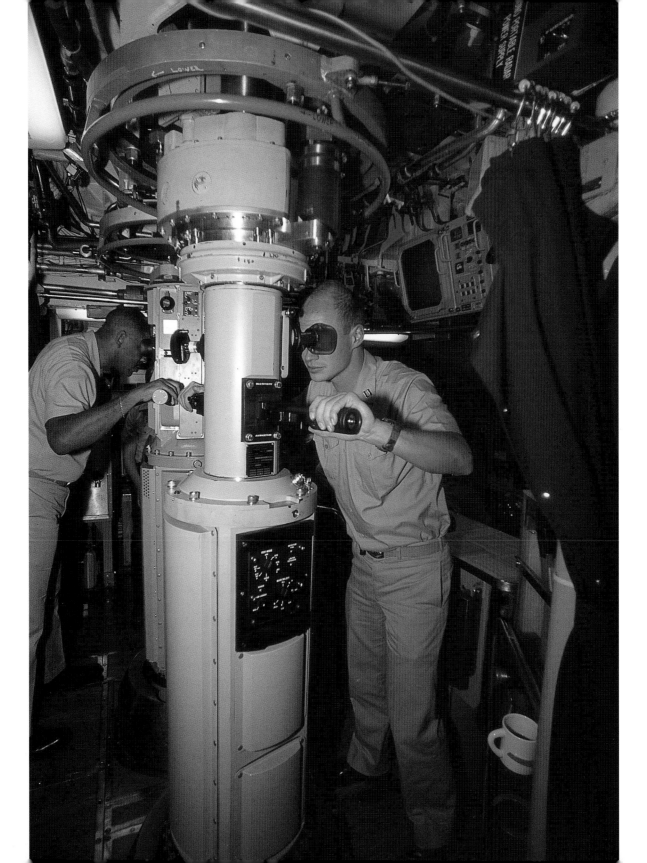

A quartermaster works at one of the plotting tables. The young sailor at the right is probably one of the "new guys." There are no Dolphins stitched above the left shirt pocket of his dungarees.

filling, flour, jelly, coffee, and more. The freezer is packed according to what will be needed, when. Special cool storage areas are for fresh vegetables and lettuce, which may last up to 30 days, depending on where the boat is going.

The food supply for a Trident patrol will weigh in at about 75,000 pounds. All food is weighed for the Dive Officer, who will need this information to compute and correct ballast for the initial embark. Upon return, they will still have about 14,000 pounds of food left over—it's a requirement to never run out of food (or coffee). Some mess chiefs are able to plan a spectacular halfway-night meal: Alaskan King Crab, Prime Rib, and Lobster Tails.

To help him, the Mess Chief might have a few Food Service Attendants who do the "grunt work," like bussing tables and cleaning up. This is a thankless job carried out by young sailors who have not yet qualified for their Dolphins. It is, however, a very important job. Since food is ranked as the number one morale booster, a Food Service Attendant who does a good job can really make a difference. A night baker makes bread, cakes, pies, cookies, and muffins from scratch. Other things made from scratch include soup and gravy. Food is stored everywhere on the submarine—any available

nook and cranny is jammed with food, as long is it doesn't present a safety hazard.

## Privacy & Recreation

There's not much privacy on a submarine. Over one hundred men work, stand watch, eat, and hang out together in relatively confined quarters. The only real place to be completely alone is in your rack. On Trident submarines, enlisted men berth together in groups of nine. The beds, or "racks," are stacked vertically in threes, like bunk beds (the middle one is best—easy to get in, easy to get out). Each rack rests on top of a storage area about 3 inches deep—you lift your bed up like the lid on a long, flat box—this is where you store personal effects like magazines, books, candy, or clothing. There are three additional storage lockers and one closet. These berthing spaces are wedged in the missile compartment, between the gigantic tree-trunk-like missile tubes.

On fast attack submarines, up to 39 enlisted men are housed in each of the sub's berthing compartments. But, there may not be enough individual berths for each man onboard. In this case, the most junior members of the crew must "hot bunk"—share a bunk—with another shipmate. When one guy comes off watch to sleep, his bunk partner will be getting up to go to work and the bunk will still be warm.

On Trident submarines, the crew has its own lounge area in addition to the crew's mess. There are also specially equipped study hall areas, each cubicle fitted with a monitor and keyboard for computer-based training programs. On the smaller, fast attack submarines, crew members study in the crew's mess (unless a movie is being shown) or find a quiet corner somewhere else on the boat in any of the many cubby holes created by the arrangement of machinery and weapons.

Officers berth together in groups of three to a stateroom. Three racks are stacked vertically. There are two pull-down desks and storage lockers. Depending on which department heads reside in the

The fire control team tracks targets at these consoles located in the Control Center. This process is known as TMA, Target Motion Analysis. The BSY-1 system automatically routes information from sonar to fire control. Variables of speed, bearing, and distance from the target are used to calculate a solution. BSY-1 can track more than one target at a time. Manual tracking is conducted simultaneously on plotting tables. Crews are evaluated on how well they can locate, identify, track, fire upon, and hit a selected target.

BSY-1 Sonar Consoles on USS JEFFERSON CITY (SSN-759). Sonar Technicians monitor the visual patterns on their screens to identify possible targets within range. Information is fed to sonar from several types of sonar equipment mounted on or deployed from the submarine. A spherical sonar array located in the bow has both active and passive modes. A low-frequency passive sonar array is also in the bow. A towed sonar array consisting of 2,600 feet of cable drags hydrophones far behind the submarine. An acoustic intercept receiver warns the crew if active sonar is being used to track their position. When sonar picks up a target, the information is routed to the fire control party.

Chief of the Boat, Rick West (left), chats with the topside watch on the deck of USS PORTSMOUTH (SSN-707). The man standing the watch wears working blues, a white "dixie cup," and carries a weapon and radio. This Third Class Petty Officer is a Sonar Technician—the symbol under the white eagle on his left sleeve depicts a set of headphones threaded by an arrow. The COB jokes that the PORTSMOUTH'S hull number, SSN-707, means "Saturdays, Sundays, Nights—7 days, 7 nights, and nothing in between."

stateroom, it may also be equipped with a telephone and other electronic monitoring systems that can be viewed without running out to the Control Center.

Favorite pastimes on board include movies, board games, cards, and reading. All submarines carry huge selections of the latest new movie releases, including the all-time favorite movie, "Animal House." Some other favorites include "Caddy Shack," "Happy Gilmore," and "Executive Decision." Action-Adventure, Blood & Guts, and Stooge Humor are the preferred genres among submariners.

Most submariners are enthusiastic readers. Science Fiction is currently very popular, although all forms of writing are consumed by members of the crew. In a chow line of twenty guys, it's not unusual to have nineteen of them with their noses in a book. Most submarines have a ship's librarian who tries to keep enough titles on hand to satisfy all crew members.

Getting enough physical exercise is one of the biggest challenges for crew members who want to stay fit. Trident submarines have extra square footage to accommodate a tread mill, rowing machine, or other piece of compact fitness equipment. In addition, the Missile Compartment provides an excellent jogging area. Attack submarines, however, offer no such luxuries of space.

Submariners are a tight-knit group and the sacrifices they make for their country are enormous. The biggest one is remaining out of contact with people back home while out on patrol. They can write letters, but there's no place to mail them. There's no phone to pick up to see how everyone's doing. The only contact a submariner may have with his loved ones comes in the form of a 50-word Family Gram—similar in length, content, and form to an old-fashioned telegram.

Family Grams are written by family members, screened by Navy personnel, and transmitted periodically by satellite. Sometimes the brevity of the message itself can cause problems—so, how much did that new car cost, anyway? She didn't mention such-and-such; what's wrong? Sometimes a message might get lost en route due to a transmission malfunction. But

USS CHICAGO (SSN-721) returns from a 6-month deployment. Crew members (except for the two divers) wear dress blues in honor of the occasion. The traditional red, white, and blue Hawaiian lei is draped over the sail. With only 130 or so men aboard, the crowd on the dock is small, but enthusiastic. There seems to be little media coverage, and what little there is may not even make the evening news.

the guy on the receiving end doesn't know that; he just knows he didn't get a Family Gram that day.

This level of isolation and separation creates mental stress for submariners out on patrol. Fortunately, submariners have each other to rely on for support and encouragement. This patrol will eventually come to an end. The day will come when their submarine will glide quietly into port, a traditional homecoming lei draped over the sail. There won't be many television news crews on hand, but those who count will be there waiting.

This has been a quick look at today's modern U.S. submarine Navy. Despite a new openness, much of what goes on remains classified. Retired submariners do not discuss their Cold War missions, and today's commanding officers observe the same code of silence. Outsiders will never hear some of the world's greatest sea stories, because those things are not discussed. One can only imagine.

# INDEX